Jack London on the Road

The Tramp Diary and Other Hobo Writings

Jack London on the Road

The Tramp Diary and Other Hobo Writings

Edited by

Richard W. Etulain

Published by
Utah State University Press
Logan, Utah

Jack London on the Road:
The Tramp Diary and Other Hobo Writings
Copyright © 1979 by Milo Shepard
Published by Utah State University Press, Logan, Utah 84322
Printed in the United States of America

Library of Congress Cataloging in Publication Data

London, Jack, 1876-1916.
  Jack London on the road.

  I. Etulain, Richard W. II. Title.
PS3523.046A6 1978   818'.5'209   78-17039
ISBN 0-87421-098-4
ISBN 0-87421-100-X

For Dad and Mom

Contents

Preface

Biographers of Jack London emphasize his trip to the Klondike and his voyages to the Pacific as notable events in his life.[1] On the other hand, his tramp trip across the United States in 1894 has not been stressed. Though London contended on several occasions that his road trip was the turning point in his life, only his second wife, Charmian, and his daughter, Joan, have discussed at length his tramp experiences.[2] Even less space has been devoted to London's attempts to use his hobo travels in his essays and fiction. By overlooking this central event in London's life and by omitting discussion of his endeavors to utilize the trip in his fiction, interpreters of London have narrowed the meaning of his career and have failed to illuminate a significant facet of his cultural milieu.

---

[1]See, for example, the first-rate study by Franklin Walker, *Jack London and the Klondike: The Genesis of an American Writer* (San Marino: The Huntington Library, 1966). During the 1950s and early 1960s Walker worked on what was to have been the definitive biography of London; the project was never completed, and he deposited his working notes and a typescript, first-draft version of London's early years at the Huntington Library. I am much indebted to Walker's thorough research (Franklin Walker Papers, Henry E. Huntington Library, San Marino, California [hereafter HEH]).

[2]Charmian London wrote the most extensive study of London's life in her two-volume biography, *The Book of Jack London* (New York: The Century Company, 1921). Joan London's *Jack London and His Times: An Unconventional Biography* (New York: Doubleday and Company, 1939) is much more analytical than Charmian's biography, and Joan provides the fullest treatment of her father's involvement in social and economic issues of his times. Less dependable on London's tramp experiences is Richard O'Connor, *Jack London: A Biography* (Boston: Little, Brown and Company, 1964), and least helpful because it contains too many errors and unsubstantiated assertions is Irving Stone, *Sailor on Horseback: The Biography of Jack London* (Cambridge: Houghton Mifflin Company, 1938). Leon Ray Livingston, known widely as the tramp A-No. 1, published a totally unreliable yarn in *From Coast to Coast with Jack London* (Erie, Pa.:

Jack London on the Road attempts to remedy these oversights. The present collection includes the first complete printing of London's tramp diary.[3] In addition, all of London's fiction, essays, and other writings dealing with his tramp experiences are reprinted here — except his book, *The Road* (1907), which has been recently reprinted. The "Introduction" includes a summary of the trip of 1894, commentary on London's writings about hoboes, and a discussion of American attitudes toward tramps in the early twentieth century. Each essay and story in the anthology is prefaced with information about its creation and publication.

I should like to acknowledge the aid of those who have helped in the preparation of this volume. Several years ago Dr. Mary Washington of the University Press of Utah State University suggested that I prepare the tramp diary for publication. She has continued to encourage me through several years of delay. A. J. (Jeff) Simmonds, archivist at the Merrill Library at Utah State, provided microfilm copies of the original diary (on deposit at Utah State) and facilitated my research in the Jack and Charmian London Collection at Logan.

The staff of the Henry E. Huntington Library and Art Gallery

A-No. 1, 1917). Throughout the present study, I have relied heavily on the volumes by Charmian and Joan London and Jack London's account in *The Road* (New York: Macmillan, 1907; Peregrine Press, 1970). The strengths and limitations of the major biographies of London are discussed in Richard W. Etulain, "The Lives of Jack London," *Western American Literature,* XI (Summer 1976), 149-164.

In some of his writings, London made sharp distinctions among tramps, hoboes, and bums; but in most of his fiction and essays he tended to use hobo and tramp interchangeably. I have followed the latter practice. For further comment on these terms, see the useful discussions in Frederick Feied, *No Pie in the Sky: The Hobo as American Cultural Hero in the Works of Jack London, John Dos Passos, and Jack Kerouac* (New York: The Citadel Press, 1964), which is also the best source of comment on London's writings about tramps.

[3]Charmian reprints extensive sections of the tramp diary in Chapter X in the first volume of *The Book of Jack London.* Nearly all the diary is published, without editorial apparatus, in "Tramping with Kelly through Iowa: A Jack London Diary," *The Palimpsest,* VII (May 1926), 129-158; the same sections of the diary under the same title appear in *The Palimpsest,* LII (June 1971). The second printing contains useful comments about Kelly's Army extracted from Iowa newspapers.

in San Marino, California (especially Ray Allen Billington, Senior Research Associate) has been very helpful. Those acquainted with the riches and rewards of research and writing at the Huntington will understand my gratitude to that marvelous haven for scholars. A Huntington Library Fellowship for the summer of 1974 allowed me to examine the largest of the Jack London manuscript collections housed at the Huntington.

More recently, the Idaho State University Research Committee and the American Philosophical Society supplied much-needed funds to carry out my research for this project and for other studies of western literary history currently in preparation. The ISU Research Committee also provided financial support to help defray costs of printing and publication.

Several years ago the National Historical Publications and Records Commission sparked my interest in historical editing by supplying a year-long fellowship to work with the Daniel Webster Papers at Dartmouth College and then gave me a refresher course during the summer of 1974 at the University of Virginia. I am grateful for these encouragements.

Over the past four years conversations with Earle Labor, Jon Yoder, Carolyn Willson, Russ Kingman, Clarice Stasz, and Alan Jutsi have stimulated my thinking and writing about Jack London. In addition, Labor and Kingman read the manuscript and saved me from several factual errors.

The staffs of the Jack London Room of the Oakland Public Library and the California State Library in Sacramento and Peter Harstad, Director, and Michael Gibson, Administrative Assistant, of the State Historical Society of Iowa have helped me track down scattered facts about the tramp trip of 1894.

Lastly, I owe thanks to the late Irving Shepard and to his son, Milo Shepard, executors of the London Estate, for allowing me to reprint copyrighted London materials and to cite pertinent manuscript correspondence.

November 1977   Richard W. Etulain
Pocatello, Idaho

Introduction

The chronic discontent that plagued Jack London throughout his life erupted again in early 1894. After quitting his job shoveling coal at a street-railway power plant, he was at loose ends, as were many working men of the time. The Panic of 1893 had swept over the country, causing thousands of bankruptcies and wiping out millions of jobs. San Francisco and Oakland were in the clutches of the Panic, and numerous workers were without employment and ready to take up with any movement of discontent that arose. Like London, they needed little urging to join Charles T. Kelly of San Francisco who was organizing his Industrial Army and announcing plans to meet General Jacob Coxey for a massive march on Washington, D. C. London decided to go east with the Army, but Kelly, under strong pressure from an anxious Oakland police force, left the city in the early morning hours of April 6th.[1]

---

[1]In addition to the items mentioned in the notes to the "Preface," I have relied on the following for information about the role of Kelly's contingent in Coxey's Army: the contemporary account by Henry Vincent, *The Story of the Commonweal* (Chicago: W. B. Conkey Company, 1894); Donald L. McMurry, *Coxey's Army: A Study of the Industrial Army Movement of 1894* (Boston: Little, Brown and Company, 1929). Early accounts about tramps and hoboes in the United States — accounts that London knew and used — are Josiah Flynt [Josiah Flynt Willard], *Tramping With Tramps: Studies and Sketches of the Vagabond Life* (New York: The Century Company, 1899); and Walter A. Wyckoff, *The Workers: An Experiment in Reality: The East* (New York: Charles Scribner's Sons, 1897), and *The Workers: An Experiment in Reality: The West* (New York: Charles Scribner's Sons, 1898). London dedicated *The Road* to Flynt, whom he considered "the real thing, blowed in the glass." He expanded his judgments on the two writers in a letter to a young writer who had also done some tramping:

> Wyckoff is not a tramp authority. He doesn't understand the real
> tramp. Josiah Flynt is the tramp authority. Wyckoff only knows the

As London's tramp diary reveals, he also left Oakland on Friday, April 6, 1894, but twelve hours after Kelly and aboard a passenger train. When London and his chum, Frank Davis of Oakland, arrived the same evening in Sacramento, they found that Kelly had already passed through the California capital. Thereafter, London took to the road; each evening he hopped an eastbound passenger or freight train and rode it through the night or until he was ditched. Beating his way across the long, cold stretches of Nevada and Utah, he finally caught up with the tail end of the Industrial Army — the "Reno Push" — on April 17th at the Ames Monument atop the Continental Divide. Two days later the Reno detachment united with Kelly's main force near Council Bluffs, Iowa.

London was in no great hurry. Two years earlier at sixteen he had undergone his first adventures as a "gay-cat" (greenhorn hobo) by "decking" a train in Sacramento and riding it over the Sierras into Reno.[2] Now he seemed bent on gathering new experiences. He had already shown interest in becoming a writer, and he appeared convinced that a few months riding the rods would allow him to garner fresh materials for essays and stories.

During the next few days after London joined the Army, Kelly and his men moved slowly through the small towns of western Iowa and reached Des Moines on the last day of April. There they were stranded because the railroads refused to move them farther. Then the Army decided to build a series of flat-bottom boats to float down the Des Moines River to the Mississippi. The

workingman, the stake-man, and the bindle-stiff. The profesh are unknown to him. Wyckoff is a gay cat. That was his rating when he wandered over the States.
(*Letters from Jack London* . . . , edited by King Hendricks and Irving Shepard [New York: The Odyssey Press, 1965], p. 126. Hereafter cited as *Letters.*)
Two useful accounts of tramps by a sociologist are Nels Anderson, *The Hobo: The Sociology of the Homeless Man* (Chicago: University of Chicago Press, 1923), and *Men on the Move* (Chicago: University of Chicago Press, 1940). Kenneth Allsop has written a lively treatment in his *Hard Travellin': The Hobo and His History* (New York: New American Library, 1967).

[2]Charmian is mistaken when she writes that the Sacramento experiences occurred in 1894, *The Book of Jack London,* I, pp. 150-153.

entries in London's diary for these days are the most extensive of his two-month journal. He gloried in his return to the water. He celebrated the anti-social activities of his comrades who disobeyed orders, pushed ahead of the remainder of the Army, and lived high off the cream of the food supplies intended for the main force. His actions during these April days confirm the report of one officer who several years later argued that London traveled with the Army but was not an integral part of it.[3]

The continual problem of finding sufficient food for the large Army and rumors that Coxey was having numerous difficulties in the East seemed to undermine the morale of Kelly's contingent. London and several of his fellows grew tired of the delays and decided to abandon the Army. On May 25th, in Hannibal, Missouri, they deserted Kelly to march to the beat of their own drums. Four days later London was in Chicago. After picking up his mail, which included money from his family, and visiting the famous White City of the Columbian Exposition, he rented a room and enjoyed the comfort of his first bed in two months. Then he crossed Lake Michigan to visit his mother's sister, Mary Everhard, in St. Joseph, Michigan. Aunt Mary immediately took a liking to Jack; she listened to his hobo yarns, read his diary and notes, and encouraged him in his dream of becoming a writer. Her sons reacted otherwise; they felt their cousin from the West was lazy and took advantage of their mother's hospitality. Later, Jack used the name of one of his cousins, Ernest Everhard, and some of the scenes near the Everhard home in his novel *The Iron Heel*.[4]

After spending several days in Michigan, Jack returned to Chicago and caught a train for New York City. He devoted a week to exploring the city, visiting historic spots, taking in tourist attractions, and lounging in parks. His reactions to the city were ambivalent: he was intrigued with the rush and variety of urban life but distressed by the poverty, alienation, and depression evident

---

[3]George Speed, who served as leader of a contingent of men from Sacramento, told an acquaintance that London "never actually joined the army, but merely traveled around or along." William McDevitt, *Jack London's First* (San Francisco: Recorder-Sunset, 1946), p. 7.

[4]Joan London, *Jack London and His Times*, pp. 82-83.

throughout the metropolis. In later years, he avoided New York because, as he said, it brought out the worst in him, and he felt oppressed whenever he visited there.[5]

One of the sights Jack did not want to miss was Niagara Falls. So late in June he hopped a train to Buffalo and visited the Falls. Then the most significant event of his road trip took place. While on his way to a second visit to the Falls, he was arrested as a vagrant and quickly sentenced to a month in jail. His experience is tersely recorded in the books of the Erie County Penitentiary of Buffalo:

> On June 29, 1894, one John Lundon [sic], age 18: Single: Father & Mother Living, Occupation — Sailor; Religion — Atheist; — was received at the Erie County Penitentiary, for a term of 30 Days, charge of Tramp, sentenced by Police Justice Charles Piper — Niagara Falls, New York; and was released on July 29, 1894.[6]

Following his release, London headed southeast aboard the Western New York and Pennsylvania Railroad. On the Susquehanna River near Harrisburg, he encountered a Negro who had also been incarcerated in the Erie prison. They laughed, joked about their experiences in Buffalo, and played several hands of cards. These brief moments of relaxation were in sharp contrast to what London experienced earlier in the day. Coming upon a group of gypsies he witnessed one man horsewhip his sons and his wife, who had tried to stop the whipping. This scene was burned into London's memory, and he set it down vividly more than ten years later in *The Road*.

Then he was on to Washington, D.C., where he stayed about two weeks. He visited as many historic spots as he could, and when his meager funds dwindled, he took a job in a livery stable. But, most of all, he would remember the city as an impossible place

---

[5] Nearly all of London's biographers mention his distaste for New York City. See especially Sydney (Australia) *Catholic Press,* January 14, 1909, Scrapbook #9, p. 118, Jack London Papers (JLP), HEH.

[6] Quoted in Franklin Walker, *Jack London and the Klondike,* p. 29. For a general treatment of tramps in the state of New York, consult Paul T. Ringenbach, *Tramps and Reformers, 1873-1916: The Discovery of Unemployment in New York* (Westport, Conn.: Greenwood Press, 1973).

to beg a pair of shoes; he had to head north out of the Capital before he was successful in finding footwear.

By the middle of August, London was on his way farther north. In Baltimore he spent several days listening to professional tramps arguing philosophy, economic theory, and revolution in Druid Hill Park. These men impressed London with their learning and their ability to converse in esoteric language about a variety of subjects. Their debates convinced him that he ought to plan his reading and that he must gain more education.

Working his way up the East Coast, Jack returned to New York City where the feelings of oppression he had sensed earlier in the summer flooded over him again. Quickly he moved on to Boston. Arriving in early September, London spent several days discovering the glories of the Hub. With a new acquaintance he traded views on capitalism, Marxism, and socialism. These were new ideas for London, and he enjoyed the opportunity to debate with his hobo friend.

The cooling New England nights were a reminder that he had to head west before winter set in. Grabbing a "virtuous couch in room 88, 888 (blind baggage) first floor Hotel de la Boston and Maine," as his Boston acquaintance put it, he headed out of Boston.[7] He passed through Lawrence, Massachusetts, and was especially watchful of "shacks" and "bulls" (railroad brakemen and policemen) as his train moved toward Vermont. He had heard that many tramps were arrested on unfounded charges in the Granite State and were sentenced to hard labor in the Rutland Quarries.[8]

Two weeks into September, London was in Montreal ready for a quick trip across Canada. He found his rod-riding slow and

---

[7]Eugene J. M. McCarthy to Jack London, October 19, 1894; this letter is pasted into the first edition of *The Road* on deposit with London's library at the Huntington Library. It is the earliest manuscript letter to London that this writer has encountered.

[8]London wrote a Vermont correspondent: " 'They have quarries in Rutland, haven't they. About 13 years ago I tramped through to Vermont, coming up from Boston. The nearest I got to Rutland was White River Junction, and there I had a narrow escape from being 'pulled in.' I understood at the time that tramps were getting 90 days in the quarries.' " Unidentified Rutland, Vermont, newspaper, February 23, 1907, Scrapbook #8, p. 92, JLP, HEH.

undependable; it took six days to travel the 120 miles from Montreal to Ottawa. On the way out of the Canadian capital, after spending a frustrating and fruitless day looking for a handout, he challenged crews of several trains and, according to his lively account in *The Road,* was able to outwit all of them. Then he landed a ride in a coal car and enjoyed his plush accommodations for the next thousand miles with intermittent stops at division points.[9]

In western Canada he met George Smith, a young tramp who traveled with London "for a week or more" through the province of British Columbia. Smith's remembrances, written forty years later to London's daughter Joan, provide a few vague glimpses of London at the close of his tramp trip. Smith remembered Jack as being choosy about his traveling companions, as one who did not "take up with every gink." Besides regaling Smith with tales about his experiences aboard the *Sophia Sutherland* (the sealing schooner on which London sailed as an able-bodied seaman for a few months in 1893), he "spoke feelingly of his colored Mammy who took care of him in his tender years." And Smith noted that Jack was "very much engrossed in taking notes and collecting data with which to write articles for the papers at his home."[10]

London took leave of his companion when Smith went south at Mission, British Columbia, and Jack traveled on to the West Coast. London enjoyed Vancouver because, as he told a friend six years later, he "was never given a handout there in all the time I slammed gates — always was 'set down' to tables. I was only refused twice, and both times because I came out of meal hours. And, further, at each of said places I was given a quarter of a dollar to make up for the refusal. Fine town? Eh? What do you

---

[9]In *The Road* (p. 122) London confuses the dates of his leaving Montreal when he cites October as the ninth month.

[10]George S. Smith to London, May 30, December 27, 1905, Box 54, JLP, HEH. Joan London (*Jack London and His Times,* pp. 89-90) draws upon Smith's letter to her, January 31, 1938. Notes on this letter are contained in the Franklin Walker Collection, HEH. The "colored Mammy" was Mrs. Virginia Prentiss who served as London's wet nurse when he was a baby and who later befriended him and loaned him money on several occasions.

think? Though I suppose the tramps have since worked it out pretty well."[11]

After remaining a few days in Vancouver, London hired on as a coal stoker aboard the *Umatilla* in exchange for his passage to San Francisco. He returned home late in September or early in October, having been on the road for six months.

Throughout his literary career, London rarely overlooked an opportunity to utilize his life in his writings. And so shortly after arriving home, he began using his tramp experiences in his fiction. Early in 1895, convinced that he needed more formal education, he enrolled in Oakland High School, and during his months as a student he wrote several stories for *The High School Aegis,* the school paper. Two of the stories, " 'Frisco Kid's Story" (February 1895 and "And 'Frisco Kid Came Back" (November 1895), deal with his life as a teenage tramp.[12]

The tales are more notable for London's use of dialect and local color than for well-formed plots and skillful characterizations. " 'Frisco Kid's Story" centers on the Kid's conversations with a man gathering information about a road kid named Charlie. Frisco tells the man how he and his friends initiated Charlie into the ways of the road. But one day when they all went swimming Charlie disappeared, and several days later his body was found downstream. When the man breaks into tears at this news, Frisco realizes that he is talking to Charlie's father. The man gives the Kid $5.00 for the information, and at the end of the story Frisco and his pal Leary Joe race off to catch the next freight out of town.

The structure of "And 'Frisco Kid Came Back" is also that of a conversation. Frisco Kid (one of London's "monicas" or nicknames while he was on the road) is reunited with a group of his young tramp partners after being gone for a few weeks. He tells them about his saving a man from drowning and about how the man, overcome with gratitude, adopts Frisco as a son. The man

---

[11]London to Elwyn Hoffman, undated but enclosed with a letter dated June 17, 1900, Elwyn Hoffman Letters, HEH.

[12]For further information on the two Frisco Kid stories, see the headnote on p. 61.

and his wife labor to clean up Frisco's manners, language, and dress; and all the time he is as uncomfortable as an atheist at a revival meeting. He dislikes the daily Bible reading and stuffy family life. Finally, he dares the neighbor kids to take a generous dose of snuff because he "Had to do somethin' fer excitement." Frisco says of the results: "Say! Yer outen seen dem kids. W'en I called time, dere wuzn't one left on de fence. Yer'd t'ink de cholera'd struck de town de way dey all chased home, sick" (p. 3). Finally Frisco escapes and rejoins his pals.

One easily recognizes parallels between the experiences of Frisco and Huck Finn. Like Huck, Frisco Kid runs away from adults who are trying to "sivilize" him. Both of London's stories draw heavily on his road experiences recorded in his unpublished diary and events that are utilized later in *The Road*. On occasion, he seems interested in suggesting more than surface details reveal, especially when he pictures the road kids as casual about stealing and stoical and even hardened in the face of death. Most of all, however, these two yarns demonstrate a young author searching for a mode in which to cast his road experiences, for a manner in which to relate some of his ideas, and for techniques by which he can communicate the impact of his observations. London wrestled with these problems throughout his career when he wrote about his tramp travels.[13]

In the next two years London prepared two other pieces about tramps. The first of these, an essay titled "The Road," was submitted to the San Francisco *Examiner* in 1897 and rejected while he was in the Klondike in 1897-98. When London returned, he tried three other newspapers — all three turned down the essay — but it was finally accepted by *Arena* for $10, $10 in subscriptions, and 12 copies of the article. London was so certain of the essay's being published that he told a reporter of its acceptance, but soon thereafter a letter arrived saying the article was " 'unavailable under amended policies of new owners.' " "The Road" was

---

[13]The most recent commentary on London's high school stories is James E. Sisson, ed., "Jack London's Articles and Short Stories in *The* (Oakland) *High School Aegis*," *The London Collector*, III (December 1971).

then retired to London's bulging files of rejected stories and essays and not published until 1970. The other piece, "Worker's Tribute to the Tramp," was lost in the mails some time in 1899 or 1900.[14]

In "The Road" London states that the life of the tramp is not sufficiently known and that his essay will clear up many misunderstandings about hobo life. Though many people have seen tramps and even met an occasional man of the road, few persons know much about the tramp, his life, and his *argot* (lingo). Frequently the tramp is considered a vagabond, a "Vag" for short. As London points out, just three letters "stand between him and the negation of being. He is on the ragged edge of nonentity" (p. 312).

Then London discusses the caste system among tramps. At the top is the "Profesh." He never works because he knows, from years of experience, how to beg, how to cajole others into paying his way and providing him with clothing. He is the "aristocracy" of the tramp world and is to be feared most because he may become a hardened criminal to keep his status. Next down the ladder is the largest class, the working tramps. They are often called "Bindle Stiffs" because they carry their "bindle" (blanket) and travel the cycle of crop harvests — wheat, hops, and berries. The most despised of the tramps is the "Stew Bum," who, London says, has often been caricatured in contemporary periodicals and is too often seen as representative of all tramps. "He is not supremely wicked nor degraded: deep-sunk in a state of languorous lassitude, he passively exists. . . . His one ambition, his one dream, one ideal is stew" (p. 314).

Others defying class categorization are the "Alki Stiffs," who seem to live on cheap gin and water. They travel in groups and frequently die young from drinking too much of the "white line" that eats up their bodies. Many tramps are cripples, having lost

---

[14]"The Road," *Jack London Reports: War Correspondence, Sports Articles, and Miscellaneous Writings,* edited by King Hendricks and Irving Shepard (Garden City, N. Y.: Doubleday and Company, 1970), pp. 311-321. "Worker's Tribute to the Tramp" was submitted to *Iconoclast* (December 4, 1898), *The Western Press* (March 24, 1899), and *Class Struggle* (April 20, 1899) before it was "among the missing" in the mails. "No. 1. Magazine Sales. From 1898 to May 1900," Box 19, Jack and Charmian London Collection (JCLC), Utah State University Library, Logan, Utah (USU).

an arm or leg in an accident. They usually roam in pairs and try to enlist a "profesh" as a protector. They have a curious fascination about each other's injuries and spend hours telling of their misfortunes. As London remarks, "One touch of amputation makes all cripples kin" (p. 315). London was sufficiently interested in this facet of hobo life to deal with the theme of cripples and story-telling in his last short story about tramps "The Princess."

For the most part "The Road" is a straightforward and uncritical essay, but London does preach a bit when discussing the "Road-kids." He says: "Saddest of all, is the training school of the 'Road' — it gets the innocent youth and corrupts them." One senses London's growing interest in Herbert Spencer's Social Darwinism when he says that it is the "modification of environment" that damages the newcomers. Only the most courageous survive, and they become hardened; the weaker ones are destroyed, often violently through accidents. Those who survive have served their apprenticeship in the jungles of competition and are now ready to become the new "profesh."

"Rods and Gunnels" (*The Bookman*, XV [August 1902], 541-544) is also an attempt to counter what London considered misleading comments about tramps in contemporary newspapers and magazines. This essay reveals London's disgust with the misinformation that "gay-cat" (greenhorn) journalists and sociologists were passing out to the public. He argues that these imposters know little about tramping in the West, where train crews are more "horstile," and these writers are also unacquainted with road lingo. They do not know basic facts like the differences between "gunnels," the connecting metal trusses beneath a freight car, and "rods," the stabilizers beneath passenger cars. London dramatizes these dissimilarities by relating his harried experiences riding gunnels and rods. Then he states explicitly:

> The point of this article is: *that when the lesser local tramps are themselves ignorant of much of the real "road," the stray and passing sociologist, dealing only with the local tramps, must stand in corresponding ignorance* (p. 543).

The falsifiers do not understand the differences between the "profesh" (or "comet"), the "gay-cat," the "bindle stiff," and the "stew bum." They are not likely to learn easily, either, for the "profesh" do not talk much to newcomers until questioners prove they too know the ways of the road. The "profesh" are "the aristocracy of the underworld"; they have demonstrated they are the fittest in the struggle for survival. As London points out: "They are the lords and masters, the aggressive men, the primordial noble men, the *blond beasts* of Neitzsche, lustfully roving and conquering through sheer superiority and strength" (p. 544). Until tramps or writers equal the knowledge and experience of the "profesh," Americans will not know what tramp life is really like.[15]

Neither "The Road" nor "Rods and Gunnels" is particularly well written, but they are of adumbrative importance because the material that London discusses in these essays — the vocabulary, the types of tramps, and the varieties of hobo life — is utilized in his later work. Once London had presented the facts of tramp life, he seemed ready to use this factual material in fiction or to point out in his articles what the existence of tramps in American society meant to people in the United States. Before he accomplished either of these goals, however, he wrote two other brief items dealing with his road experiences.

In May of 1900, the same month that London's first collection of stories was published, the Boston *Evening Transcript* printed a short piece by London entitled "Jack London in Boston: Reminiscence by the Author of the 'Son of Wolf.'" The essay is unlike most other things London wrote about his tramp travels. It is neither fiction nor an expository essay; it is merely a reminiscence, a joyful remembering of things past and was probably printed to help advertise *The Son of the Wolf,* which was being published by the Boston firm, Houghton Mifflin and Company. Most of all, the essay reminds one of the humor and vivacity of some sections of *The Road,* London's only book-length publication about his tramp experiences.

---

[15]One editor complained that "Rods and Gunnels" was too much a "correction, rather than a general treatment of the subject." He felt that London had not woven his subject matter into a "narrative and episodic form" and that the essay lacked "individuality." J. O' H. Cosgrave (Doubleday, Page and Company) to London, December 18, 1901, Box 13, JLP, HEH.

London begins by recounting his leaving New York and heading for Boston. Along the way the "shacks" (train policemen) give him a great deal of trouble until he hides in a gondola. There he reads the newspaper and sneaks in a nap. Then a "shack" discovers him and acts as if he will terminate London's free ride. As London puts it,

> I was in imminent danger of being forcibly ejected from a moving train. Such things are not pleasant; so I bandied words with the man, criticised his general make-up, and dissertated upon the vascular action of the heart and the physiological cataclysms caused by intemperate anger. I also commented upon his ancestry and blackened his geneological tree. As behooved a tramp of parts my mastery of intensive adjectives and vituperative English was such as invariably to move men in my direction (p. 32).

The man accepts London's verbal challenge, but once he enters one end of the large pipe London inhabits, he has lost his advantage. London crawls out the other end and hits "the grit" on his own power.

Soon thereafter he arrived in Boston. It was early September. He talked his way out of trouble with the police by spinning yarns about his seagoing experiences in the Far East. He later wandered about the Boston Common and got lost — for the only time in his life, he claimed. Then he encountered a southern college man who was also tramping in Boston, and they spent several days in Charleston near the Bunker Hill monument. "Here we took sunshine," London wrote, "and talked Karl Marx and the economists." They also discussed Kant and Spenser and enjoyed one another's company. But they parted because London had his eye "fixed upon Montreal and Ottawa, and winter was coming on."

The other item London tossed off with iittle effort was a nineteen-line poem entitled "The Worker and the Tramp: A Villanelle" (*The Comrade,* I [October 1901], 14). It is a heavy-handed attempt to show the paternalistic attitudes of many workers toward tramps. London suggests that laborers do not realize that a gift of money — "Here's a quarter to spend" — is inadequate to repay the debt workers owe men of the road; but his diction, his forced rhymes, and his explicit irony spoil his point. Judging from this poem alone, one can not claim much for the poetic talents of London.[16]

Before he began to write sections of *The Road* in late 1906 and early 1907, London turned out three other prose pieces dealing with his tramp life and the impact these events had on his outlook. The earliest of these essays, "How I Became a Socialist," was published in *The Comrade*, II (March 1903), 122-123. In this essay London shows how his tramping experiences converted him from Nietzsche's ideas of the blond beast to the concepts of socialism. He had always been an individualist and a strong believer in hard work, but when he saw what hard work had done to many honest men and how they had suffered, been maimed, and driven to the road, he changed his mind. He writes: my "rampant individualism was pretty effectively hammered out of me, and something else as effectively hammered in" (p. 123). After leaving the road, returning to California, and reading about labor problems in the United States, he realized that he had been converted to socialism. Throughout this essay, the emphasis is on London's personal experiences and how these activities shaped his later life.

"The Tramp," which appeared in three parts in *Wilshire's Magazine* in February through April of 1904, is the most technical and propagandistic of London's writings dealing with tramping. He argues that the capitalistic society contains a surplus labor force and that the tramp is a "by-product of economic necessity" (p. 71). Whenever workers strike, there are more than enough "scabs" to take their places, but when all jobs are taken (which is the usual situation) there are still large numbers of men who wish jobs but can not find any. Some workers are unfit and inefficient so they easily become unemployed, but others simply are unable to find an employer who needs a working stiff. And thus it is the unfit and fit alike who are forced to the road. To avoid the daily disappointments and embarrassments of unemployment and to escape the abyss they have fallen into, they become tramps.

---

[16]Early in his career London wrote numerous poems, but none betrayed impressive poetic talents. This poem is his only verse to deal with tramps.

These new men of the road revel in their freedom and do not realize that in taking to the road they make secure the jobs of other men, women, and children. While the tramp is not "an economic necessity such as the surplus labor army, . . . he is the by-product of an economic necessity." For the capitalist society, the road becomes a safety valve "through which the waste of the social organism is given off." Moreover, the tramp is playing the "eunuch's part" in the twentieth century: "He does not breed. Sterility is his portion."

London completes his essay with a sarcastic yet sympathetic paragraph about the tramp's plight. Americans ought to allow the tramps to clutter the highways and train yards; tramps should not be forced or even encouraged to go to work. If they are and do, persons currently employed will be thrown into the army of the jobless, or a monstrous army of would-be workers will pull down society. The hobo is a hero; he allows America to continue: "we should give him credit," London writes. "Let us be just. He is so made. Society made him. He did not make himself" (p. 191).

"What Life Means to Me" (*Cosmopolitan Magazine,* XL [March 1906], 526-530) does not emphasize London's tramping days. Instead, he reviews his philosophy of life before the spring and summer of 1894, and then he summarizes what his thoughts and acts were after his return from the road. The tramp east in 1894 and the things he saw, London says, "gave him a terrible scare" (p. 7). When he viewed the "cellar of society, down in the subterranean depths of misery," he could no longer hold to his philosophy of individualism; he began to doubt that the work ethic, that capitalism, that survival of the fittest were ideas he wished to champion. Instead, he began asking questions about the American system and decided that he would avoid the abyss that many men had fallen into. He realized that using his mind could keep him from the miserable situations that he had seen. "So I resolved to sell no more muscle, and to become a vender of brains."

At the same time that London was trying to publish his essays he was writing several short stories about tramps. Most of his articles were eventually accepted for publication, but editors rejected his first hobo fiction, and it was not until 1903 that he sold his first story about tramps. "Local Color" (*Ainslee's,* XII [October 1903], 74-82) concerns a loquacious tramp named Leith Clay-Randolph, who is modeled after London's tramp friend, Frank Strawn-Hamilton. Clay-Randolph comes to visit the narrator and panhandles him for food, clothing, and a bed while he spins a yarn about his experience writing a newspaper article. Clay-Randolph lives up to his impressive name. Though a tramp, he is a philosopher and an erudite man who has read widely and seen much of the world.

In spite of the interesting story that Clay-Randolph tells, "Local Color" is not a strong work because London fails to practice what he had preached. As he told his good friend, Cloudsley Johns, a writer must allow his characters to dramatize their personalities; he can not *tell* his readers, he has to *show* them. And in this case Clay-Randolph is an unbelievable protagonist because London does not allow him to act out his character. Moreover, the plot line is too skimpy. It is merely the story that Clay-Randolph tells with a few additional questions and comments by the narrator.

The story is notable, however, for its revelation of the problems London faced in trying to use his tramp experiences in fiction. A number of significant questions arise about London's treatment of his experiencs. What would be his attitude toward his materials? How could he deal with the social and economic problems that had made such an impact upon him after 1894? How was he to create a tramp hero? Would his readers allow him to make the tramp an heroic figure? "Local Color" suggests some interesting if incomplete answers to these questions.[17]

Clay-Randolph tells the narrator that when he commenced his story about tramps the newspaper editor warned him not to emphasize social, economic, or philosophical commentary. Instead, he should stress dialect and humor; he ought to produce a sketch of

---

[17]Feied, *No Pie in the Sky,* pp. 23-34, comments on the merits of London's stories and essays about tramps. Kingsley Widmer discusses the varying roles of tramps, hoboes, and rebels in recent American literature in his *The Literary Rebel* (Carbondale, Ill.: Southern Illinois University Press, 1965), pp. 91-139.

15   *Introduction*

"local color." This was the same advice that editors gave London; he should either portray the tramp as a kind of picaresque hero, or he should take the stance of an objective reporter and describe the life of the tramp without picturing too many dreary (and certainly no ugly) details. Unlike the cowboy figure in Owen Wister's *The Virginian* (1902), the tramp could not be a "hero" because he was not sufficiently genteel to be made into an heroic character. So "Local Color," though not a first-rate piece of fiction, is noteworthy for what it reveals about the barriers facing an author who wished to write serious fiction about tramps.

London once remarked that writers draw from two sources for their stories: their own experiences and the lives and books of other writers. London's next tramp story, "The Apostate," (1906) was, in part, a product of personal experiences. It relates the story of young Johnny who has had to work since he was seven to support his mother and his family. Most of the story details his year-after-year struggle to keep working and his gradual disintegration as a reflective person. One day he becomes sick and lies in bed for several days. He realizes what is happening, and he decides to become an "apostate" by walking away from his job and taking to the road.

London intends this story as a case study of what causes young men to become hoboes. If the available description of London's life prior to his becoming a tramp in the spring of 1894 is true, he experienced some of the frustrations of young Johnny. It is the beastly, meaningless, and numbing work that impels teenage boys and young men out of the factories into trampdom. They go knowing what their absence may mean to their families' pocketbooks and dinnertables but also knowing that they must get away if they are to keep their identity — and their sanity.

"The Apostate," like "Local Color," is primarily a sketch. And London is again guilty of telling more than he shows; there is little character development and too much sentimentality and propaganda. Yet it is a persuasive picture of why young men become hoboes. There are revealing glimpses of the guilt complexes that London must have experienced when he turned tramp.

He too faced the conflict between the financial needs of his family and his desire to find himself.[18]

Shortly after completing *The Iron Heel* in the late fall of 1906 (the novel was not published until 1908), London began his most extensive work on his road experiences — the nine essays first published in *Cosmopolitan Magazine* and later collected in book form as *The Road* (1907). Although London had been urged on earlier occasions to use his tramp days as the basis for a full-length volume (and he had expressed willingness to do so), a specific set of circumstances caused him to begin the tramp series late in 1906. First, he was having difficulty placing *The Iron Heel* as a serial, and he needed funds to pay his large daily expenses. Second, he was in debt to *Cosmopolitan* because he had not yet written the material for which he had been given a handsome advance. But now the journal was willing to accept a series of tramp articles for the balance due them. Finally, he badly needed additional money to pay for the mounting expenses involved in building the *Snark,* a boat on which he expected to make an around-the-world cruise. The last of these pressures bore heaviest on London in late 1906.[19]

The urgency of the moment determined the manner in which *The Road* was written. London turned out enough words to pay off his debt to *Cosmopolitan,* and then he continued the series to gain more money for his spiraling expenses. He was never clear on how many essays he planned, in what order they would be written, and what subjects he would cover. The pieces betray his lack of planning and his tendency to spin yarns rather than to emphasize the form of his tales.

Most of the nine sections of *The Road* deal with enough specific incidents that they could have been arranged chronologically to give the full impact of his travels. But when the book

---

[18]In the best study of London's literary artistry, Earle Labor (*Jack London* [New York: Twayne Publishers, 1974], pp. 23-24) makes a case for considering "The Apostate" as "emotionally, if not literally, autobiographical" (p. 23).

[19]Charmian London explains some of these financial pressures in a letter to Elwyn Hoffman, February 28, 1907, Hoffman Letters, HEH. London details some of his worries in *Letters,* pp. 233-245. All his biographers deal with his financial woes in building the *Snark.*

was published, London was satisfied to have the episodes placed in the unplanned order that he wrote them rather than to have them organized in such a manner as to give the full impact of his experiences. Two essays, "Road-Kids and Gay Cats" and "Confession," deal primarily with his earliest tramp travels in 1892. Two others, "Hoboes That Pass in the Night," and "Two Thousand Stiffs," center on his escapades with Kelly's Army. " 'Pinched' " and "The Pen" treat his days in the Erie County jail. His travels from Buffalo to Washington, D.C. and northward to New York City are delineated in "Pictures" and "Bulls"; and "Holding Her Down" is a lively account of his outwitting train crews while on his way westward across Canada.

It is not surprising that the individual sections of *The Road* are primarily narrative and anecdotal in form. London, who seemed unable to cast his hobo materials in an extended narrative, chose to lard the individual essays with episodes and yarns to illustrate a few generalizations. This approach gives *The Road* a folksy appeal but also contributes to its lack of unity. For example, the first section of the book, "Confession," opens with a story about London's lying to a woman in Reno in 1892. Then he tells of his experiences in Reno, returns to the woman, relates his failures to land a handout, describes a man who stubbornly refuses to give him food, reverts to the Reno woman, goes on to points about his story-telling abilities, and finally back to the woman in Reno. All of the nine segments are organized in similar fashion: London begins with an idea, gets sidetracked on different stories or experiences, and then returns to where he began. Judging from the hand-written manuscript of the book on file at the Huntington Library, he followed his usual practice of quick composition with little or no revision before publication. Had he chosen to structure his experiences and to examine more closely his reactions to his tramp travels, he could have enlarged the meaning of his book.[20]

---

[20]In editing *The Road* for publication in 1967, I. O. Evans, an Englishman, rearranged sections of the book so that they follow chronologically London's tramp experiences. Notice the differences between the two formats:

Macmillan, 1907	*Evans, 1967*
Confession	Road-Kids and Gay-Cats

But these criticisms can be carried too far. Although *The Road* lacks unity and contains surprisingly little social commentary, it is an entertaining book. London knows how to tell a story, and *The Road* illustrates his abilities as a raconteur. He catches the joy, the adventure, and the youth of his tramp days. In words similar to the mood of Ernest Hemingway's *A Moveable Feast,* London writes at the end of one of his many episodes: "The day was done — one day of all my days. To-morrow would be another day, and I was young" (p. 73). Joan London is correct when she summarizes her father's experience in writing *The Road:* "Fatigued by the strain of writing *The Iron Heel,* and in the midst of the harassments which accompanied the building of the Snark, Jack escaped happily into the past, reliving his adventures as he set them down in clean, vivid prose."[21]

Four years elapsed before London placed another piece about his tramp life — this time with the *Saturday Evening Post.* "The Hobo and the Fairy" (CLXXXIII [February 11, 1911], 12-13, 41-42) opens with Ross Shaklin, a hobo, sleeping under a bridge. He is unshaven, dirty, and smeared with blood, and obviously suffering the aftereffects of a drunken spree. He is a human wreck ready for the scrap heap.

Then little Joan appears. She finds Shaklin, chases away the flies swarming around him, and uses her umbrella to shield him from the hot sun. He awakens to find her hovering over him, and at first he thinks she is a fairy unacquainted with the evil things of life, things that have beaten him and left him in the place where he lies. Through careful choice of words, London aptly describes the hellish appearance of the hobo and the Edenic atmosphere that radiates from little Joan and her nearby home. Shaklin tries

---

Holding Her Down	Hoboes that Pass in the Night
Pictures	Two Thousand Stiffs
"Pinched"	Holding Her Down
The Pen	Pictures
Hoboes that Pass in the Night	Bulls
Road-Kids and Gay-Cats	"Pinched"
Two Thousand Stiffs	The Pen
Bulls	Confession

[21]Joan London, *Jack London and His Times,* p. 328.

to relate the terrible ordeals he has been through and why he is now a hobo, but the little girl, though listening to what he says, tells him that he must change his mind, get up, and try again. He resolves to do so.

London implies that Shaklin's chance meeting with little Joan (who is the same age as London's daughter Joan) and the impression she makes on him in a few minutes is sufficient to change his ways. Though he has spent many years as a tramp and has been involved in several criminal acts, she has the power to transform his life in a few moments. London's treatment of Shaklin's sudden conversion is not persuasive, and one wonders why the *Post* bought the story except that it exchanges a gloomy beginning for a happy ending. London's hobo is a Bret Harte hero with a rough exterior but a golden heart, and all that is needed to reveal his real character is to have it disclosed by the goodness of little Joan. London did not work hard on the tale, and this lack of effort is evident.

Published two years after London's death in 1916, "The Princess" is his last piece of fiction to deal with tramps — and the strangest of his hobo stories. Three older tramps, each minus an arm, gather in a hobo jungle. Each has his "alki" to drink, and each takes turn telling a tale. All three are interested in explaining their lives and how each has lost an arm — one to a shark, one to a pulp grinder, and the third in a dynamite explosion. The tales of the first two alki tramps include a princess who, Beatrice-like, spurs on the tale-teller. The third tramp forgets the part about the princess and then tries to slip her in near the end of his yarn. The other two leave him quickly and exclaim "No gentleman would have done it."

This brief summary is not an injustice to London. The story includes the meeting of the three hoboes, their drinking, and their brief tales. It does contain materials about "alki" hoboes, crippled tramps, and reveals the raconteur abilities of the "comets" that London describes in his earlier essays; but little of importance is suggested in the story, and thus it is the weakest of his fictional pieces about his road life.

At this point one must ask: Why did London have so much difficulty producing first-rate fiction about his tramp travels? There seem to be two answers to the question. In the first place, London was attempting to use a character who was an unacceptable fictional hero to many Americans. Just as many readers objected to the uncouth cowboy as a hero until he was romanticized in the 1890s, so many editors would not publish fiction dealing with tramps in the years immediately before and after 1900. The hobo was not an inspiring subject for teenage girls and coffee-table books — two of the unrefutable tests for measuring acceptable fiction in the last years of the nineteenth century.

London's attempts to publish his writings about tramps illustrate this problem. Few leading magazines of his time were willing to publish material about tramps, although essays and sketches were more acceptable than fiction. Included among the hundreds of rejection slips that London received are several from editors unwilling to accept short stories about hoboes.[22] And at times London was advised not to write non-fiction about tramps. Such is the case when he tried to publish his tramp essays in book form as *The Road.* His editor and publisher, George Brett of Macmillan, and his close friend, George Sterling, thought the collection of tramp reminiscences would diminish the sales of his other books because readers would regard *The Road* as a glorification of the hobo. Both Brett and Sterling argued that London ought to deal with more uplifting subjects than the life of the tramp.[23] As John

---

[22]For further information on rejection and acceptance of London's tramp writings, see the headnotes before each item reprinted in this collection.

[23]The correspondence between Brett and London and Sterling and London on this matter is extensive. Brett first wrote an encouraging letter to London about doing a book-length study of tramps (Brett to London, January 23, 1907, Box 9, JLP, HEH). Then, after seeing a manuscript copy of *The Road,* he was "doubtful" about the project (Brett to London, February 28, 1907, Box 9, JLP, HEH). After London's reply, Brett enlarged on his reservations and included a copy of a letter to the editor of a New York newspaper criticizing the sections of *The Road* that had appeared in *Cosmopolitan;* again London answered Brett with strong reasons for his writing and wanting to publish *The Road* (London's answers are printed in *Letters,* pp. 241-242, 245-246). Finally, Brett agreed — from a financial perspective — that London was correct in wanting the volume published (Brett to London, August 14, 1907, Box 9, JLP, HEH).

Seelye has pointed out, Americans in the early years of the twentieth century were not yet willing to embrace the hobo as a hero,[24] and in attempting to treat the tramp in fiction London was crashing headlong into the barrier of public opinion. In this case, his cultural milieu was nearly as impenetrable as a brick wall.

A second reason that London failed to write important tramp fiction may be the result of another problem mentioned above. When he found that his stories about hoboes were rejected, he wrote sketches and essays about his road experiences and awaited a more propitious atmosphere in which to place tramp short stories and novels. He planned to use the tramp figure in several pieces of fiction, but in writing the essays that were included in *The Road* he seems to have squandered most of the raw materials intended for his subsequent tramp fiction. London's experiences on the road were now more than a dozen years in the past, and he sought new adventures on which to base his fiction.

Another limitation hampered London's efforts to write superior hobo stories: he was unable to produce a full-bodied tramp character. None of his works includes a convincingly-portrayed hobo. And the notes that he left behind for other tramp projects indicate his future tramp stories might have suffered from the same weakness. London's hoboes philosophize, speak in dialect, and spin yarns; but they are not actors. They do not live the characteristics ascribed to them, and their actions do not personify the ideas that London claimed to have garnered on his road trips. If London's contemporaries were reluctant to accept the tramp as a hero, he never proved that he could create a persuasive hobo figure. His failure to turn out powerful tramp fiction, then, seems as much the result of his artisic shortcomings as the result of his bucking a culture hostile to tramp fiction.

One must ask, moreover, how much impact did Jack London's

---

[24]John D. Seelye, "The American Tramp: A Version of the Picaresque," *American Quarterly*, XV (Winter 1963), 535-553. Another good essay on tramps is Clark C. Spence, "Knights of the Tie and Rail — Tramps and Hoboes in the West," *Western Historical Quarterly*, II (January 1971), 5-19, which is reprinted in revised form and with illustrations as "Knights of the Fast Freight," *American Heritage*, XXVII (August 1976), 50-57, 92-93, 96-97.

tramp experiences have upon his thinking? If one accepts at face value all that London said about the subject, the trip of 1894 was a turning point in his life. For example, in his essay "How I Became a Socialist" (1903), London argued that his tramp adventures revealed how the other half lived, how the "submerged tenth" was recruited. On the road he saw what society was doing (and had done) to men who had had his strength and youthfulness and that these men were now broken humans. These sights scared him, and he vowed never to be trapped by the forces that had ruined so many men and had driven them from their jobs, their homes, and to the road.

Three years later he wrote in "What Life Means to Me" that his hobo meanderings had thrust him into "the cellar of society," into "the abyss, the human cesspool, the shambles and the charnel house of our civilization." And, he added, "the things I saw there gave me a terrible scare." He determined not to become a victim of this depressing situation, to go back to school, and to "become a vender of brains." After he studied his surroundings and articulated his dissent, he found that his friends called his ideas "socialism," although, he says, he was not aware at the time that his views were a part of a well-known ideology.

Yet there are other indications that London's tramp trip did not have the large impact on his life and thinking that he contended. Nowhere in his unpublished diary, for example, are there illuminating comments on social problems. London is more interested in describing the comaraderie he enjoys with the other men. The predominant tone is one of merriment and adventure — the joyful jaunt of an eighteen-year-old in search of experience and acquaintance with other men and their varied backgrounds.[25] Throughout his life, London experienced these same kinds of urges; they sent him adventuring on board several ships, tramping through

[25]Franklin Walker comments on the lack of social commentary in the tramp diary in "The Tramp" section of his incomplete typescript biography in the Walker Collection, HEH. Most of London's notes for stories about tramps that he never wrote are contained in a folder titled "Leith Clay-Randolph," Box 97, JLP, HEH.

Korea, and the Klondike, and speeding through endless lists of books and ideas.

When London turned out his most extensive work on tramps — *The Road* — he did not choose to include lengthy commentary on social issues. Except for a brief section on prison life, London stressed primarily the colorful and entertaining details of tramp life rather than material dealing with social and economic problems.[26] There is the possibility that London avoided the pose of the social critic to ensure the sale of the essays, but correspondence between London and the editors of *Cosmopolitan* does not confirm this possibility.[27] More convincing is the conjecture that by 1907 London simply may not have been interested in exploiting the social and economic dimensions of his tramp experiences in non-fiction, just as he had not been and would not be in his fiction.

One must conclude that though London claimed his tramp trip had profound impact upon his life and thinking, he did not transmit the profundity of the experience into his fiction. In addition, his non-fiction dealing with his hobo travels is not first-rate. Why were London's tramp writings not among his best work? Why was he not able to produce writing about his road experiences that matched the high quality of his works on the Klondike? Was it that editors and readers were reluctant to accept the hobo? Did he lack sufficient

---

[26]Later in his career, London wrote about his remembrances of prison life in *The Star Rover* (1915). When a man questioned him about his information, London told him that everything in the novel was true and based on men's experiences in prison. Then, he added, "If you ever read a book of mine entitled *The Road,* in which I give some few of my experiences, you will notice that in the Erie County penitentiary at Buffalo, New York, I have slipped by without describing much of the worst that I found obtaining there. What I found there was unprintable, and almost unthinkable." London to Max Ehrmann, December 2, 1915, Box 69 JLP, HEH. Notice, too, that the photographs of prison life in the first edition of *The Road* are particularly inoffensive. No picture contains prisoners, and no scene depicts anything especially depressing. Perhaps Brett was able to tone down what he considered the offensiveness of *The Road* by omitting pictures that might displease sensitive readers.

[27]London to *Cosmopolitan Magazine,* January 1, 2, February 21, March 5, 7, 1907, Box 69, JLP, HEH. *Cosmopolitan* to London, December 27, 1906, January 8, 11, February 7, 21, 1907, Box 13, JLP, HEH. These letters contain no disagreements except those concerning differing word counts.

artistic versatility to portray believable tramp heroes? Probably both of the last two questions must be answered affirmatively.

Despite the artistic shortcomings of much of London's work about tramps, these writings are important for other reasons. First of all, even though London's tramp experiences brought about less sensational and less abrupt changes in his life and thinking than he indicated, they did bring recognizable modifications. As Earle Labor has pointed out, London's hobo days "sharpened his story-telling ability," they "tempered his naively individualist attitude and started his questioning of the American socio-economic system," and finally they helped him to realize that he must "use his brain rather than his brawn to make his way in the world."[28] Generally, his eyes were opened to sights and experiences that had previously escaped him, and he realized that some of the purposes of his life would have to be rethought and probably redirected.

London's works about tramps also demonstrate his life-long tendency to dramatize his personal experiences in his fiction and essays. His adventures in the Northland with miners and natives were worked into such novels as *A Daughter of the Snows, The Call of the Wild, Burning Daylight,* and numerous short stories. He drew upon his voyages aboard the *Sophia Sutherland* and the *Snark* for *The Sea-Wolf* and the *South Sea Tales,* and his experiences in prison and with various radicals helped him to write *The Iron Heel* and *The Star Rover.* Moreover, his planning and developing of his Beauty Ranch were inspirations for *The Valley of the Moon* and *The Little Lady of the Big House.* And, most of all, *Martin Eden* is directly related to many of the events of his early life. These works, along with *The Road* and his essays and fiction about hoboes, reveal London's interests in sailors, prospectors, prisoners, and tramps — character types whom the genteel society of his time rarely considered acceptable subjects for literature.

In addition, London was the first major American writer to deal with hoboes. Later, John Dos Passos, John Steinbeck, and Jack Kerouac, among others, wrote about migrant workers and

---

[28]Labor, *Jack London,* pp. 31-32.

tramps. And there is another dimension to London's hobo writings — a dimension that indicates London's contribution to a notable theme in American literature. In the nineteenth century from Washington Irving and James Fenimore Cooper to Mark Twain, authors dealt with Americans' tendency "to light out for the territory ahead of the rest." And after 1900, writers continued to fill their novels with characters who take to the open road. Indeed, as Sam Bluefarb asserts,[29] we have been preoccupied with flight, and thus the escape motif is a key theme throughout our literature, particularly in American writings of the twentieth century. Jack London's tramps and hoboes are solidly in this tradition. They desert the old for the hope of the new; they are on the move to avoid a depressing past and present and to search for a future that, while not yet clear, seems to promise more than their previous life.

The largest contribution of London's tramp writings is their revelation of some of the cultural and intellectual changes that were sweeping through America in the years surrounding 1900. As many Americans became conscious of the closing frontier of the 1890s, they sought means of escaping the circumstances slowly encircling them. For some, like Owen Wister, there was escape to sections of the West that still seemed to be frontier areas; for others, like London, Hamlin Garland, Stephen Crane, and Frank Norris, there was the possibility of flight to the Klondike, to the high seas, or overseas. For still others, the road beckoned — the leaving of jobs, the fleeing from family responsibilities and pressures, and the taking to the adventure of the road. Not all who became tramps did so as a means of escape. As London makes clear, many men were forced into hobo life because they lost their jobs or were not physically able to hold positions available to them. When London dealt with tramps, he was writing about a portion of a society experiencing a closing frontier and searching for a new one. And he was the first American author to treat the hobo as a by-product of a culture gradually moving from frontier status to an urban industrial society. With more than sixty years of

---

[29]Bluefarb, *The Escape Motif in the American Novel: Mark Twain to Richard Wright* (Columbus: Ohio State University Press, 1972).

hindsight now available, we can see that London was opening a new vista through his writing about tramps. He was attempting to relate the rising number of tramps to the social and economic changes circulating through America at the beginning of the twentieth century. Many of his contemporaries — including some of his friends and editors — were unwilling to admit or face the parallels that London drew between tramps and a changing American culture. In short, although literary critics may note the artistic limitations of some of London's tramp writings, cultural historians will cite these works as significant evidence for a clearer understanding of Jack London, the man and the writer, and for a larger comprehension of the era of the closing frontier in America.

The Tramp Diary

Jack London's tramp diary was apparently written during or shortly after his trip across the West with Charles Kelly's Industrial Army in the spring of 1894. There are no large breaks in the handwriting in the manuscript diary or in the narrative, and thus one can probably assume that the diary was in its present form when London arrived in Michigan in the first week of June or when he returned to California early the next fall.

The tramp diary, which is a part of the Jack and Charmian London Collection (Box 20) at the Merrill Library at Utah State University, is recorded in a small address book whose original owner was Frank Davis of 715 12th Street, Oakland. (This is the Frank Davis who began the tramp trip with London in 1894 but who turned back after a few days on the road.) Davis' name is crossed out and replaced with "John London 1321 22 Ave Oakland California." On page three a note in London's hand reads: "This was Frank's book before I got it, and I guess you will see a good deal of his handwork, throughout. Jack."

The brief diary is five inches wide, seven inches long, and one-half inch thick and contains about seventy-three pages of text in addition to a few pages of London's notes on terms and ideas for essays and stories. Throughout the diary there are phrases and numbers in Davis' hand, but his scribbling takes up little space in the book.

London's account of his tramp trip begins one-third of the way through the 100-page diary. The narrative continues for about sixty pages, and then London returns to the front of the book to complete his final entries up to page seventy-three. Interspersed among the completed pages are blank pages and other notes.

In all, about sixty-five pages are completely filled with London's tramp diary, ten pages or so are blank or nearly blank, and the remaining pages contain other scribbled notes and numbers.

I have used the following editorial guidelines in preparing the tramp diary for publication. First of all, I have retained as much of the flavor and style of the original as possible. In doing so, I have refrained from adding *sic* whenever London misspells a word or wrenches the syntax of a sentence, and I have added editorial changes only when the meaning would be obscure without such additional material. The editor's additions or corrections are enclosed in brackets. I have not used words that have a line drawn through them, and whenever London has written over a word, I have used what seems to be the latest version of the text. When he consistently misspells a place name, I have corrected only the first misspelling.

In this transcription I have omitted a few materials in the diary that have no bearing on his tramp trip. Above all, the diary reveals that at eighteen years of age London was already a good storyteller, and I have preferred to allow him to tell his story without its being smothered in explanatory notes.

FRIDAY APR. 6.

Left Oakland Mole at 4:30 P.M. & arrived at Sacramento at 8 P.M. Went up to the Mississippi Kitchen & had supper. Learning that the Industrial Army had arrived at noon & departed for Ogden at 4   Went down & caught the 10 P.M. Overland bound East.[1]

---

[1]The Oakland Mole was a railroad station in Oakland on San Francisco Bay. It was the terminal for the Southern Pacific Railroad, and from the terminal passengers caught ferry boats at the slips located at the edge of the Mole. It opened January 22, 1882, and was torn down in 1966 (Doris Johansen, Oakland Public Library, to Richard W. Etulain, June 25, 1976). It is estimated that Kelley's Industrial Army numbered about seven hundred when it left Oakland; three hundred and fifty men joined the Army in Sacramento, and the total may have reached as high as 1,400 before the Army reached the Mississippi River. The two best sources for published information about Kelly's group are Henry Vincent, *The Story of the Commonweal,* and Donald L. McMurry, *Coxey's Army: A Study of the Industrial Army Movement of 1894.* In the margin for the entry of April 6, London writes: "Sacramento 90 mi. S.F. End Division"

SATURDAY APR. 7.

We held her down all night till we arrived in Truckee at 7 A.M. As it was broad day light it was impossible to proceed further. Tho' they were forced to stop the train twice before they succeeded in ditching us. Frank[2] & I then decided to send our valises back to Oakland by Wells Fargo. We traded the patent simple file for 4 square meals.

We tried to take the 8 P.M. Overland east, but by a mistake Frank caught her & I was left. But we had agreed that in case of separation we would meet in Wadsworth. About eleven o'clock I caught a freight out, but slept so sound despite the cold that I was side tracked at Reno without waking up. Staid in Reno all day but did not hear of Frank. In the evening

SUNDAY APR. 8.[3]

Woke up at 3:30 A.M. half froze to death. I climbed out & walked about till my circulation was restored when I sought shelter in the Restaurant. The deaf mute & the ladies edifying conversation. Morning ablutions by the banks of the Truckee River. Mourns the loss of the clothes brush & comb with Frank, but still have the towel & soap. Went down the road & watched them loading cattle & pigs. Met a Swede on the road & went & got dinner with him. Watched the Indians gambling & listened to the salvation army & unemployed congregated on the corner. They are making up an army & expect to start east to morrow. All along the line from Oakland on, we have met hundreds chasing the first detachment of the industrial army   A great many lost it by the unexpected departure so early Friday morning. Took a freight in the evening & made Wadsworth, but did not find Frank. I slept in an engine cab down in the yards & was routed out about 4 in the morning when the wipers took possession.

---

[2]The cover pages of London's tramp diary indicate that "Frank" is Frank Davis of 715 12th Street, Oakland. No further information about Davis is available. See London's entry for April 11. London writes in the margin of the April 7 entry: "Truckee 259 2/10 mi. End Division"

[3]In the margin of the April 8 entry, London writes: "Reno 294 2/10 mi."

MONDAY APR. 9.

Went down to the Post Office & received a postal from Frank who has gone to Winnemuca. Gen. Kelly[4] passed through on the morning overland. Met a Doctor who gave me unasked a quarter of a dollar & invited me to breakfast. He said my face was familiar, but we could not scrape up any recollections. Am waiting to catch a train across the desert to Winnemuca, where if I arrive on time Frank & I will join the Reno detachment of the Industrial Army & then *On to Washington!*

All along this part of the road the wipers are Chinese & the section hands, Italian I saw the biggest New Foundland in my life here to day. He looks more like a bear than anything else. It is impossible to take a train out till night for all the crews are in to me. I could catch any of them & ride them to the next stop, but I want to catch one clean through. This is the last stop before entering the desert, & I dont wish to be ditched at some lone water tank where I may pass days waiting for a train to stop. I never saw such weather. The days are burning hot & the nights freezing cold. The sky is so clear & the atmosphere so thin that you can see objects at a long distance & are deceived into believing them very close. I thought my face was sea tanned[5] but it is nothing to this. The sun

---

[4]Charles T. Kelly was thirty-two years old in the spring of 1894. Born in Hartford, Connecticut, in 1861, he moved west and became a newsboy and later a printer in Texas and California. He was active in union affairs in San Francisco and joined the Industrial Army soon after its organization. He was described as "a small, slight man, with mild blue eyes, a soft, winning voice, and a breadth of forehead that indicates more than average intelligence," and as one who looked "more like a divinity student or the secretary of a Y.M.C.A. organization than the commander of nearly 1500 men." The Des Moines *Weekly Iowa State Register,* April 20, 1894, quoted in McMurry, p. 152. The *Harper's Weekly* (March 5, 1894) added: Kelly "was merely a creature of circumstances and of the moment, but the caravan ought to be grateful for the luck which sent it a man of such cool judgment." Quoted in *The Palimpsest,* LII (June 1971), back cover. London writes in the margin of the April 8 entry: "Wadsworth 555 2/10 from Ogden. End Division"

[5]London is probably referring here to his recent experiences as a sailor aboard the *Sophia Sutherland,* a three-masted schooner, which sailed throughout the eastern Pacific on a seal-hunting expedition in 1893. London served nearly seven months: from soon after his seventeenth birthday on January 20 until the following September. In the margin of this entry London writes: "Wadsworth = Shortest division on the road."

has peeled the skin off my face till I look as though I had fell into a fire.

All along I have met swarms of people going east, & but one going west. I met the curiosity here this afternoon. He is walking all the way from Colorado to Frisco, where he is going to ship to sea. Then I met a Frenchman who had walked all the way from Minnesota to Sacramento & has walked this far back. Now his shoes have given out, & he proposes to ride the rest of the way
I took the 10:45 train out this evening & made her across the desert to Humbolt where I got ditched. No sooner had the Overland pulled out than an orange special pulled in. I took her out & she ran clean through to Winnemucca a distance of fifty miles without a stop. A spark caught fire in my overcoat & smoldering away suddenly burst into flames. The train was going about 40 miles an hour and it was quite a job to put it out. My overcoat & coat were ruined. I rode the bumpers the rest of the way.[6]

---

[6]Bumpers were the coupling gears between railroad cars, or a piece of timber or steel beam placed across the ends of cars, tenders, or locomotives near the coupling devices to absorb the shock of coupling or collisions. Tramps usually rode the bumpers at night when hoboes were more difficult to see and hence safe from the brakemen.

Six years after returning from his tramp trip, London wrote to a Nevada writer about some of his experiences in her state:

> I do not know much of your country, though I once beat my way up to Reno to the state fair when I was a boy, and later, I tramped through on my way east. If you lived along the railroad then I may have slammed your back gate in search of breakfast — in some of those little greasewood sagebrush towns I am sure I slammed every gate[;] my stomach or I called quits. I remember bunking three days in the round house at Winnemucca, and I pushed coal for the fireman to Carln. How do people manage to live up there? I have often marvelled over that point. And if you do scratch a living, how then do you then manage to exist? Or, are there little valleys and secluded nooks way off from the railroad where Nature smiles just a wee little bit?

Two weeks later he added:

> Tell me; is the Humboldt House between Wadsworth and Winnemucca? If so, I was put off there one midnight, from the Overland, and pulled out half an hour later on a fast freight.

(Jack London to Idah Meacham Strowbridge, June 2, 17, 1900, Elwyn Hoffman Letters, HEH.)

TUESDAY APR. 10.[7]

Arrived at four o'clock & waited till daylight in the European restaurant. Frank's postal said if not in sight to call at the La Fayette Hotel. Did so but no one knew him   Then examined the post mark on the postal card & made out San Francisco. It look bad for some body. If I had not delayed at Wadsworth & here I would have been almost to Ogden. About 9 o'clock went down to Post Office & wrote a letter home. As I was returning met Frank. Great rejoicing & congratulations. The post mark inexplicable. Frank & I decided to wait this night out in the hopes of joining the Reno detachment. But two trains came through.

WEDNESDAY APR. 11.

It snowed last night. We have decided to let the Reno crowd rip & start on as fast as possible for Ogden.

This afternoon Frank & I had an understanding. The road has no more charms for him. The romance & adventure is gone & nothing remains but the stern reality of the hardships to be endured. Though he has dicided to turn West again I am sure the expearience has done him good, broadened his thoughts, given a better understanding of the low strata of society & surely will have made him more charitable to the tramps he will meet hereafter when he is in better circumstances.[8]

He starts West & I start East to night. He is safe to go through because he has money enough to tip the brakemen on the line at the rate of 50 cts. a division & have money left to eat on. Shook hands & said good bye at 9 P.M.

Caught a freight out. Am going to brake coal on the engine from here to Carlin 131 miles.

THURSDAY APR. 12.

Arrived in Carlin at 3:30 this morning. A little railroad town situated in the midst of the great American Desert, through which

[7]London writes in the margin of the April 10 entry: "Winnemmucca 475 4/10 mi. S.F. End Division"; at the top of the page, he adds: "Sand Storm."

[8]These references to Frank's decision to leave hoboing are one of the few times in the diary that London comments about the "values" of tramping.

I am now traveling. Up to two o'clock no train has passed east except the Overland. I met a Chinaman here & played cards with him while he was waiting to register. There was not a game he did not understand. I took the overland out about 7:30 riding the blind with two other fellows I picked up with. We made a 45 mile run to Elko & a 23 mile run to Peko where they tried to ditch us. We went out ahead but the brakeman rode the blind out. We waited till the train had almost run by when two of us jumped the palace cars & decked them while the third went underneath on the rods. I climbed forward two cars to the other fellow & told him to come on along the decks to the blind but he said it was too risky.[9] I went forward about five cars & as the brakeman was on that platform I could proceed no further & escape observation. I waited & when the train stopped I climbed down & ran ahead to the blind. The brakeman again rode her out but I took the next one behind him, & when he jumped off to catch me I ran ahead & took the platform he had vacated. The fellow on the roof with me got ditched, but I made her into Wells, the end of the division where they put on a double header. The brakeman was after us like a blood hound so I climbed on the engine & passed coal through to Terrace, the end of that division. I arrived at two o'clock, & as the snow was all around, I did no[t] care to proceed further so I went to the round house & slept in the cab of an engine till morning.

FRIDAY APR. 13.

At five this morning the wipers took possession of my bed room & I was obliged to vacate. While looking for another warm

---

[9]A blind refers to a railroad car — usually a baggage car — with doors only on the side. Access to the blind was from between cars or down from the deck. The palace cars were usually passenger cars, sleepers, or diners. Decking was the dangerous trick of climbing quickly from the bumpers or blind to the roof of a moving car. The rods were the connecting iron bars beneath a passenger car. About eighteen inches separated the rods from the bottom of the car, and it was in this cramped space that the tramp frequently found his free accommodations. In the incident mentioned above, London and his companions were forced to deck the car or ride the rods because the brakemen occupied the blind. But notice that London outwitted his opponent by running alongside the train to another blind nearer the engine. He tells of several such incidents in "Holding Her Down," *The Road*, pp. 24-52. London writes in the margin of the April 12 entry: "Carlin. 535 mi. S.F. End of Division"

spot I found that two Knights of the road, arriving during my sleep had most obligingly built a roaring fire in one of the huge stoves. One of them had a big handkerchif full of fresh buttered, home made biscuits. I sat down, ate a few of them & then slumbered peacefully till seven o'clock. The further I got east in Nevada the more miserable the towns are, & Terrace is commencing to the upward scale I guess, for at last I am in Utah. At two this afternoon I got one of the west bound tourists to lock me in a car bound east. Just before the train started the door was thrown open & a brakeman asked me how much I could "shake up." "Fifteen cents" was my response. I had two dollars & fifteen cents on me and as the two dollars were unbroken I did not propose to give them to him. He said he would carry me down the road a ways, but did not take the money. When we had traveled about 50 miles, according to my calculations, the door was again thrown open, & the conductor & brakeman both appeared. After a long consultation the[y] took my gold ring & left me the fifteen cents. The ring was good gold with a fine cameo setting. I got it from Lizzie Connelen.[10]

SATURDAY APR. 14.

Arrived here [Ogden] at 12:50 this morning. Took a stroll up town, & got supper, then another stroll & at half past two wandered into the Central Hotel where I took a stiff drink and sat, by the night clerk's permission, in a chair till daylight.

Ogden is a pretty little town of 18000 inhabitants. It has all the latest improvements. Electric cars, & lights, & bituminous rock. It is situated at a good elevation among the Rocky, or rather the Wasatch Mts. which are outlying spurs or ranges of the rockies. One surprising thing is the cheapness of everything. Strolling

---

[10]Irving Stone spells Lizzie's last name Connellon (p. 52). He says she "worked with a hot fluting-iron in an Oakland laundry." Stone adds: "Lizzie had a pretty face and was fast on the saucy comeback; she gave Jack her gold ring with a cameo insert to show that he was her feller" (p. 44). Charmian London (p. 165) refers to her as Lizzie Connolly and points out that she is treated in *Martin Eden*. In the opening, unnumbered pages of the tramp diary, London gives her name as "Lizzie Connellon, 1020 — 3 st." In the margin of this entry, London writes: "Terrace 123 Og. End division" and "In this car had a horrible dream."

Jack London in 1902, at the time of his trip to London.

A tool from Kelly's Army used in construction of flat boats at Des Moines, May 7, 1894.

"My ticket used by me, in 1894, when tramping," the notch rested on truck of the four-wheel, passenger coaches.

Jack London in 1904 with his husky "Brown Wolf" during the writing of The Sea Wolf.

An encampment of Kelly's Industrial Army 1894 (from The Book of Jack London, *Vol. I, p. 161*), courtesy of the State Historical Society of Iowa, Iowa City, Iowa. Jack London is in right hand corner.

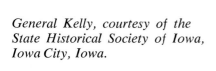

General Kelly, courtesy of the State Historical Society of Iowa, Iowa City, Iowa.

Frank Strawn-Hamilton, Jack London's tramp-philosopher friend. (All photographs, unless otherwise noted used by the courtesy and permission of Russ Kingman, Milo Shepard and the Jack London estate.)

Lunch near Shelby, courtesy of the State Historical Society of Iowa, Iowa City, Iowa.

through the town I noticed several log houses which must have been built during the early days. Another peculiarity is that so many of the living houses or cottages are built of brick & stone. Perhaps it is because of the deep snows during the winter. It began snowing to day in the morning but cleared up in a few hours. I have give up my proposed trip to Salt Lake City & intend to start to night for Omaha on the Union Pacific. I received 3 letters. Two from home & one from Applegarth.[11] I expected more & made arrangements with the Post Office to forward them to Omaha.

After spending a pleasant afternoon in the reading rooms I went down to the U.P. Depot & caught the blind baggage[12] on the 8:15 Express. Just as she was pulling out I met an old friend. We first met in Reno when he & I spent the day together. He is a Swede. We next met in Winnemucca. He arriving just as I was leaving. And now for the third time we met while catching the blind baggage. We rode her 75 miles that night to Evanston, a pretty little town just across the line in Wyoming. After we had run a few miles he pushed coal on the engine. About this time the brakeman began to stir us up. There were quite a crowd on the blind. But gradually, station by station they began to drop off. How ever I made up my mind to hold her down & a pretty time I had of it. I rode the blind, the tender of the engine, the cow catchers & pilots of the double header, the decks & even in an emergency once stood on the platform in the middle of the train. We arrived in Evanston at 12 P.M.

---

[11]The Applegarth family played a large role in London's early life, especially in the years after he returned from tramping until his first marriage in 1900. Ted Applegarth introduced Jack to his sister Mabel, who was three years older than London. He soon fell in love with Mabel, and they might have married had Mrs. Applegarth agreed to the match, but her Victorian gentility and pride of family never allowed her to accept London as a possible son-in-law. Mabel became the model for Ruth Morse in *Martin Eden*. It was through the Applegarths that London met Bessie Maddern, his first wife. London writes in the margin of this entry: "Ogden 833 miles from Sacramento End of Division. End of S.P.'s line & Railroad center of U.P./S.P./ & Denver & Rio Grande."

[12]Most writers refer to the blind baggage as the space between the locomotive and tender and the first baggage car. The car immediately behind the tender usually did not have a forward end door, and hence this spot was a favorite site for tramps to hide from railroad policemen. London writes about his experiences with blind baggages in *The Road,* pp. 29-52.

SUNDAY APR. 15.[13]

The train stopped at Evanston for half & hour, then ran back to Ogden & came around by the Oregon Short Line. The cause was a bad wreck, 11 miles ahead. Coming round a bend through a cut the engine ran into a huge bolder which had fallen on the track. The engine jumped the track on one side killing the fireman & engineer. A tramp was riding the blind & he jumped off & was not even injured. The baggage & mail cars fell on the opposite side The rest of the train was pretty badly shaken up. About 1:30 an engine brought in the two bodies. The Swede & I went over to the electric light works, & going down into the fire room crawled up on top of the boilers & slept till morning, though the heat was intolerable. The snow covers the ground walks & houses yet though it is rapidly melting. It took but a few hours to patch up the track & by ten o'clock the Swede & me. (By a queer coincidence his name is also Frank.) captured an Orange Special Through Freight. We rode her the best part of the day & when she stopped at Green River the end of the division, & 111 miles east of here we left the train for a few minutes to get a lunch. I returned with a loaf of bread and chunk of bologna sausage & made her out, but Frank did not arrive on time. They carried me but one station 15 miles, where I got ditched.

ROCK SPRINGS.[14]

It seemes to be a mining town. I went up to a Saloon, got a glass of beer, & had a fine wash in warm water. I am writing this in the saloon. It seems to be the wild & wooly west with a vengeance. The soldiers, miners & cowboys all seem to be on the rampage. At the present moment a couple of cowboys or cattle punchers are raising cain generally. One is about 6 foot 4, while the other is a little shorty. I guess I will stay here tonight & to morrow & take a look at the town & mines. This is the town where rock spring coal comes from.

---

[13]The margin of the April 15 entry carries these words: "Evanston 75 mi. Ogden. 958 mi. Omaha. End of division."

[14]In the margin London lists the population of Rock Springs as "4000 inhabitants."

MONDAY APR. 16.

I had the hardest job in the world this morning searching for the depot. There are thousands of cars laying on the side tracks waiting for coal, & trains run north, south, east & west of here. I saw a pretty sight here at school time this morning. All the girls going to school wore fascinators & knitted hoods. There was but one exception, & that little girl wore a white sun bonnet.

11'o clock A.M. A heavy snow is now falling.

I waited all afternoon, but as the trains were late I did not get out till 5:30. I caught the flyer & held her down to the next division, where I got ditched at 9:40. I stayed in Rawlins till 12:30. It was blowing a blizzard by this time & freezing cold. The saloons were all full, & poker, stud horse, faro, craps & roulette were all in full blast. At 12:30 I caught an Orange Special & climbed into the ice box of a refrigerator car, & you bet it was cold before morning. I arrived at Laramie the end of division at seven o'clock. It was so cold on the train that night tha[t] the brakemen did not care to bother me. I covered 257 miles that night

TUESDAY APR. 17. LARAMIE.

When I left the train at Laramie the snow was so thick that one could not see over a rod ahead. My feet were so cold that it took a half an hours brisk walking to restore the circulation. Had a good breakfast at the resturaunt, & at twelve o'clock, as the blizzard was at about it's worst, I caught the blind of the flyer, intending to make through to Cheyenne & in the evening make on again. But when I reached Ame's Monument the highest point on this line, I overtook the Reno Detachment of the Industrial Army. 80 strong & camped in a refrigerator car, attached to a through freight. I climbed aboard & made myself at home.[15] That night we crossed

---

[15]The Ames Monument was a huge granite pyramid erected on Sherman Hill at the summit of the Rocky Mountains in honor of Oakes and Oliver Ames, who helped finance the building of the Union Pacific. When London caught up with the Reno detachment, the major part of Kelly's Army was still several days ahead; it had arrived in Council Bluffs on April 15. Joan London, probably following an account in the unpublished diary of H. R. Lytle (a lieutenant in the Reno group and an occupant of the refrigerator car that London entered), uses Lytle's words to describe her father as a young man with "round features and dark curly hair.

the line; but it was not till we were well into Nebraska that we ran clear of the blizzard.

WEDNESDAY APR. 18. GRAND IS.[16]

Our fare for supper & breakfast was boneless ham, cheese bologna sausage, bread & crackers. At Grand Island we were taken to the Resturaunt & given a fine dinner, though we were guarded by the local police, so that none would escape. We traveled all afternoon & night & arrived at Omaha at 1 next morn.

THURSDAY APR. 19. OMAHA COUNCIL BLUFFS.
CAMP KELLY WESTON.

We arrived in Omaha at 1 A.M. & were met by a special platoon of policemen who guarded us till we were shipped over the Missouri river, into Council Bluffs & the state of Iowa. I made up my mind not to march five miles before daylight in the heavy rain out to Camp Kelly situated at Chatauqua park. When we left the cars I deserted in company with the Swede who I had lost in Green River but picked up about 40 miles to the eastward of Grand Island.

We went to sleep in a bar room which was being moved, while the army marched through the mud & storm 5 miles over the country road to Camp Kelly, where they arrived at 5 A.M. I arose at five, said good bye to the Swede, & catching a freight train, was eating breakfast in Omaha at 6. I strolled about the town, watched the new post office in process of erection, and on attempting to cross the toll bridge was stopped & sent back. I met a sympathiser who raised a quarter for me & a ride all the way to camp, where I arrived at 10:30, & joined my company. at about

---

He wore a chinchilla coat, a novel in each pocket, and cap pulled well over his head. His flannel shirt, shoes, and trousers had seen better days." He carried no blankets or extra clothes and referred to himself as Sailor Jack, although he admitted his real name was Jack London. Joan says there were 84 men in the Reno contingent (pp. 73-74). In the margin of this entry London writes: "Cheyenne 57 miles   576 mi. Omaha   End of Division."

[16]London notes in the margin of the April 18 entry: "End of Division. 156 mi. Omaha."

11 the Army was under way & countermarching before General Kelly proceeded to march 7 miles to Weston, & little town situated on the lines of the Chicago Millvaukee & St. Paul, & the Rock Island railroads. The first Regiment of the Reno Industrial Army is the Combination I march in, and am in the last rank of the rear guard. The Army made quite an imposing array, with flags & banners & Gen. Kelly at their head astride of a fine black horse presented by an enthusiastic Council Bluffs citizen. After we had marched about a mile I dropt out & helped a sick man along. He had been in the hospital at Camp Kelly & being convalascent had overestimated his strength. I carried his blankets & assisted him over the trestles. The army took the road with about 12 wagons loaded with food & camp traps. We took the short cut by the R.R. track, and he was so weak that he got dizzy & nearly fell into every trestle we crossed. Leaving him seated in a comfortable place sheltered from the rain which was coming down in torrents, I went up to the only store, country store in the town. Never did the store Keeper do such a rushing business. In 10 minutes he was out of cheese, crackers, ginger snaps and all such eatables.

In ten minutes after the army had arrived the camps were formed, fires built & dinner under way. Each company's leutenant goes to the commissary & get the rations. Though the rain sleet & hail was coming down in torrents we made quite a meal in stew bread & coffee. As the night came on the wind increased & grew bitter cold, blowing from the north. The men soon scattered in search of lodgings. The owner of an elevator gave permission to occupy it & in less time than it takes to write it, it was occupied by 300 men. I soon found a hay loft in a barn, & gradually, the men began to straggle in till it was full. By that time Kelly & officers had been out rustling & lodgings were found sufficient for all, though they were quite surprised when they found our barn full. Just as I was settled comfortably, the muffled crys of a cat aroused me & on digging, in the hay beneath my head, found a cat with a litter of kittens. A big Irishman & I pretty near had a fight. He wanted to throw them out in the storm, but I told him when he threw them out he threw me. The cat & kittens stayed. We passed a pretty comfortable night, though the Mick arose with the cold every two hours & woke me up in his efforts to get warmer.[17]

FRIDAY APR. 20. WESTON

We had a breakfast of fish, beans, sour craut, coffee & bread. Then I went to the commissary to get a pair of shoes, but they had none. My feet are on the ground. One sole is entirely off & I am walking on my socks. A special train with R.R. officials came down yesterday, & again to day. The Chicago Millwauke & St. Paul commenced to send all of its rolling stock east & train after train of empties, cabo[o]ses & extra engines flew past us, without stopping. A rig occupied by Mr. Lemon[18] of some importance in the Christian Home, drove out and arrived covered with mud, & with steaming horses telling us that the people of Omaha & Council Bluffs had risen en masse & were on their way to demand transportation for the army, of the railroad. Now and again mud covered vehicles would arrive with later news, till at last they came telling us we were to go out to night on a train obtained by the citizens & which was even then making up. Then when it was authentically affirmed the Army was ordered to obtain rations, make a hurried meal & be ready to take the train. We are the last to obtain rations as we were the last to join the army. At about 8'o'clock a head-light was seen running down the C.M. & S.P. road. In an instant all the reserve fuel was stacked on the fires, & a grand shout of rejoicing went up to the heavens. About a mile from town the train stopped. The foreman of the section and one of his men were caught in the act of tearing up the track & the man was captured, then the train slowly proceeded into town with men in advance to see that the tracks were all right. The train had been

[17]Vincent is mistaken on several details when he says of the Reno group: "Before the departure from camp Chautauqua two hundred new recruits had arrived from the west. They constituted General Gorman's battalion, which had come from Denver to Council Bluffs in a refrigerator car on the Union Pacific Road" (pp. 136-137).

[18]Rev. J. G. Lemen was the manager of the Christian Home Orphanage at Council Bluffs. Lemen operated the home, which was probably established in the 1880s, until his death in 1904.

stolen. Three Young ladies induced an engineer's son to take his father's engine.[19] A train of box cars had been picked up & loaded with Omaha & Council Bluff's citizens. How ever it was too small to accomadate the army & after the citizens & Kelly held a consultation it was decided to march back early next day to Council Bluffs where the people would get us another train. The train stopped about & hour or two & several songs were sung by the girls & boys on the engine, Mr. Lemon, wife & ladies, & the citizens & soldiers of the Industrial Army. With tootings of the engines whistle, & amid the shouts of the army the train pulled out, carrying our promise to meet them next day. A few of the boys tried to take the train in preference to walking, but were soon persuaded to rejoin their companies. I went up to the commissary where I spent the night. The commissary ducks have a fat time of it, but of course they have to work pretty hard. I obtained a blanket and as there were no shoes and it was impossible for me to walk back I arranged so as to ride back on one of the commissary wagons. It was quite a comparison to my quarters of the night before in the hay loft.

SATURDAY APR. 21. WESTON

At day break all were awake & up. The lieutenants & men from the different companies were momentarily arriving to obtain their morning's rations. Coffee sugar, bread, beans pork & jelly was served out & soon a hundred different fires were brightly burning and as many breakfasts in the different stages of completion. After breakfast a few men from the different companies started to walk back to Council Bluffs but they were overtaken and a detail placed to prevent the rest from following. After breakfast we had quite a commotion in our camp. The captain was no rustler

---

[19]Vincent (pp. 123-124) and McMurry (pp. 171, 192n) mention only two women as involved in the stealing of the train. A picture of Annie Hooten and Edna Harper is included in Vincent following page 216. Their presence with the Army caused discontent among the men and criticism of Kelly in the local newspapers. As one reporter put it, "them women" were wearing "stockings worth $2.50 a pair in spite of the fact we are on the verge of summer." Quoted in *The Palimpsest,* LII (June 1971), 309.

for his men, & they took offense at a board he had had painted in which his name Capt. Gorman[20] was conspicusly displayed. After quite an excited consultation everything was arranged satisfactorily, & the banner is to be destroyed. Then he took me up to the Comissary with 4 others & tried to get shoes but there were none. While there a private of Company B. San Francisco was tried by a drum head court martial, & on being found guilty was drummed out of camp. He was supposed to be a railroad detective, reporter or Pinkerton. The evidence was strong & he was convicted by a vote of 9 to 4. In the after noon we were visited by citizens of Leola [Neola] & Underwood who begged us to march on to their town where we would receive a hearty welcome. After we had speaking & singing we were dismissed to our camps with orders to get the mornings rations at once. The cooks to be up & commence breakfast at four; all hands to be ready at six for breakfast & camp to be broke at seven o'clock sharp. The young ladies that stole the train were present, & they could not escape without speaking. We had a pleasant time at our camp fire singing song after song & it was not till after eleven that we began to think of sleep.

WESTON UNDERWOOD LEOLA. SUNDAY APR. 22.

As soon as breakfast was over I was up to the comissary but could not obtain shoes. Every thing was in an orderly confusion. The town was turning out to see us off. Companies were marching here to there to gain their positions   teamsters & wagons were on the go; the comissary officers all life & motion; aide flying in all directions, while the wires were working and on all sides stragglers hurrying to rejoin their companies. As usual we were last in line. 6 or 7 men deserted from Company A. San Francisco & remained around their fire. Col. Baker[21] led us back on Gen. Kelly's big

---

[20]Gorman was captain of Company L, part of the Reno detachment, and the company to which London was nominally attached.

[21]Col. William Baker organized the first group of the Industrial Army in San Francisco area (Vincent says the organizing took place on April 2 [p. 126]), but his inability to lead and his uncertainties about the purposes of the Army caused the recruits to look to Kelly for directions. Baker seems to have gotten on well with Kelly until the incidents that London mentions later in the April 22-25 entries.

black horse & we took their blankets away. We had hardly got underway when I threw away my shoes & walked barefooted into Underwood 6 miles distant, where after a dinner presented by the citizens, I got a pair from the comissary. All along the route inthusiastic crowds on foot, on horses & in double rigs turned out to meet us. After a couple of hours stop we proceeded to Leola the county seat. They sent the militia out to meet us, and it was an apt comparison with the Ogden & Council Bluffs militia. A troop of little children & ladies. We marched through the town with hundreds of citizens joining in our rear to march. It was more like Fourth of July than a peaceful Sunday in a quiet little country town. We marched through the town & down a steep bluff to a picturesque spot alongside of the railroad known as Butler's Woods, where we pitched our camp. Before we broke ranks there was speaking & a welcome by the mayor of the city. We are assured of transportation by 150 farmers wagons on the next morning. As we broke ranks there was a grand scramble up the steep bluffs to a pile of wood, & in less time than it takes to write it every cord had vanished. All afternoon the ladies & gentlemen of the town thronged the camp, mingling with the boys, & in the evening there was a general rejoicing. In all the camps singing & speaking was going on the ladies mingling their sweet voices with those of the boys all hoarse from the cold weather & sleeping out nights. The ladies of Omaha & Council Bluffs were still with us with their escorts. In one portion of the camp church was held & a local minister officiated. In another about 2 score of germans sent their old country songs echoing throughout the camp. We had our own little time, the principal feature of which was songs & dances by the cook. At 10 o'clock we started to march to a stable in the town which our second lieutenant had procured for us. We were stopped by the pickets, but Col. Baker came along with quite a jag & a woman on his arm & passed us through. He will most likely be court martialed tomorrow.

MONDAY APR. 23. LEOLA MENDEN AVOCA

We had an early break fast, but were prevented from making as early a departure by an attempt to break up the Army by

Col. Baker. He was ignominiously cast out. About half of us took wagons & the other half walked. Of course our company walked. My feet were so tender I could not walk. They tried to get me into a wagon but it was no go. When Kelly came along I spoke to him. But he, not realizing my condition, & thinking I was trying to shirk told me a wagon could take my shoes for me. As I could not walk I lay down & the Army pulled through without me. By & by the city Marshall came along I [and?] tried to send me on but I told him I was going to stay in town till my feet got well. Then he hurried on to overtake the army. In a few minutes he returned with a couple of officers of the army who proceeded to bundle me into a passing wagon, & I was on my way to overtake the surgeon's wagon. Just as I climbed aboard about 30 citizen's headed by the Marshall hailed Baker & told him to take the track & head out. I rode in the doctor's wagon 8 miles to where dinner was served. We passed at 5 miles through the pretty town of Menden. All along the line it resembled a rout or retreat. The S.F. were riding in advance & all along the line the men were scattered in companies squads groups, pairs & singles. Our company had no coffee for dinner. That Afternoon we arrived in Avoca where we were taken just beyond the town to our camp. Though we looked & were tired when a cottontail was scared up hundreds joined in the chase. The rabbit had no show & was soon captured. Another & Another & still another was scared out & captured. None escaped the boys. That night we slept in a barn, where the whole company was treated to a stiff drink of whiskey before retiring.

Tuesday Apr. 24. Avoca Walnut Marne Atlantic

We were up early & underway by 9 o'clock As usual our company was walking while the S.F.'s rode. I walked 6 miles to the town of Walnut enduring the severest of tortures & I arrived in a most horrible condition. I resolved to go no further on foot. As usual our company had no coffee for dinner. Then Col. Speed[22]

---

[22]George Speed (1854-1931) had a long history of participation in reform activities — before and after his involvement in the Industrial Army. He was single, worked as a hatter, and was the commander of the Sacramento division of the army. The men from Sacramento preferred to follow Speed, and their actions

& Kelly had a row & for awhile it looked as though there would be a general fight. But it was all peacably settled. Col. Baker withdrawing with about 150 men but when they marched out both crowd were together. As usual our company walked. We had just had a row & elected as Captain our second lieutenant in preference to Gorman. I dropt out & with about ten others lay in wait to catch the first train. But the marshall getting alarmed raised the necessary wagons & bundled us into them. They carried us 8 miles to Marne the next town. All along the line it resembled a grand retreat. Pots, Kettles, frying pans coats, clothes, blankets, broken down men, & in the town a commissary wagon was stopped & the cook & doctor were unable to proceed with it till the town raised $2 for the driver. They then provided another team, but about 20 were left. At last after dark 7 of them started to walk, & as the trains went through at full speed, we still stayed. Finally an old soldier provided us with supper & teams to go on to Atlantic, 8 miles distant. We arrived between 9 & 10 & were taken to the comissary, where we had supper again. I rejoined my company & went off to bed.

WEDNESDAY APR. 25 ATLANTIC

We are to spend the day here. We are all camped in the fair grounds near the race track. Kelly has gone on to Desmoines. No He did not go. The camp was thronged with citizens all day, & in the afternoon the late troubles were all made up & Baker & Speed rejoined the army. Mr. Lemon was the prime factor in causing this reconciliation. Speed Baker Lemon, Goodspeed,[23] the Associated Press & other reporters & a noted lawer addressed the army. A Game of base ball was also in progress between the Army & Town Boys. The Atlantic boy's won with a score of 16 to 12. But the Army boys were not in condition. In the evening I ran the pickets & strolled around town. Just after I returned a

encouraged the rivalry that sprang up between Speed and Kelly. Speed was a member of the Socialist Labor Party (in whose meetings he and London would meet again after their return from tramping), and in 1905 he joined the Industrial Workers of the World and participated, says Joan London, "in every major strike" of the IWW for "almost a quarter of a century" (p. 183).

[23]Goodspeed was chairman of the citizens' transportation committee of Atlantic, Iowa.

brass band marched down & the camp was soon listening to addresses by camp orators and townspeople. Every body expresses a good opinion of the army, & a great many were surprised at the gentlemanly bearing & honest appearance of the boys

THURSDAY APRIL 26 ATLANTIC WYOTA [WIOTA] ANITA ADAIR.

We had a slight delay in breakfast by the want of bread but that was soon supplied & by ten o'clock we were under way. Pretty near all our company rode, & I did all day. At 7 miles we passed the town of Wyota, at 14 Anita where we had a dinner furnished by the townspeople, & at 22 arrived at Adair where we camped. All the trains are running, with a force of Pinkertons on & the railroad has issued circulors against the seizing of trains. As usual I ran the Pickets, & in company with one Lee saw the town & visited the hobby horses. When we returned we had quite a job to enter. All citizens had been requested to leave the camp & if any were to remain they would be arrested & sent to head-quarters. If any Pinkertons or detectives are caught it will go hard with them.[24]

FRIDAY APR. 27. ADAIR CASEY STUART

We were under way bright & early, & capturing two wagons started out ahead of the whole gang. We had a fine rustler driving our team. The old farmer & the food, sack of potatoes, & chickens. "You'd better ask the wimmen folks. Here they be." We were left by both wagons in Casey, & after quite a wait succeeded in captur-ing 1 wagon for luggage. Into which a great many of us also piled. We raised some coffee on the road & cooked a dinner in preference to driving a couple of miles out of our way to Menlow [Menlo] where a dinner was prepare by the townspeople. With a great deal of joking & fun we arrived at Stuart, having covered a distance of 23 miles. We rested outside the town waiting for the stragglers to come in before we marched through the town. Then marched through the town to camp. A double line of pickets are on duty

---

[24]Railroad detectives and Pinkerton agents infiltrated the army's ranks on several occasions, and their presence, when known, angered the men. See London's comments under the entries for May 15-16.

to night. We expect to make a forced march of 40 miles to Des Moines to morrow. As usual the camp is thronged with visitors from the town. A great many ladies are present & a few have brought baby buggies.

SATURDAY APR. 28 STUART. DEXTER EARLHAM DES SOTO
[DE SOTO] VAN METER

Were under way bright & early. Walked 11 miles through the town of Dexter to Earlham where we had dinner. My feet are in such bad condition that I am not going on any further, unless I can ride. I will go to jail first. It was impossible to get a ride, & I went down to the station. A train left at three o'clock, & playing on the sympathies of the people I raised a ticket, & was soon in Van Meter, three miles beyond De Soto. The Army is straggling in but it will be hours before the last arrives. Gen. Kelly intends to push on to Des Moines twenty miles distant. At nine o'clock in the midst of driving rain, thunder & lightening the Army received orders to march. About half started out in the pitchy darkness. We stormed the pickets stationed on the bridge & gained the town. Three of our company & about a dozen others slept in the mayors office.

SUNDAY APR 29 VAN METER. BOONEVILLE

At four o'clock we were awakened by a deputy sheriff. All the rest including my three companions walked out the rail road track. I have 8 blisters on my feet & more a'coming so I could not walk. I went down to the Coon River washed & then went to camp where I found three more of our company. About 400 were assembled & as their appetites increased they proceeded to the comissary. They had no orders to issue rations, but when we all came up in a body, they saw they had no show & we all soon had a good breakfast underway. As I can't walk I intend to stay here till transportation is furnished. Ate dinner with the Comissary Cook, & afterwards went down to the river & took a swim. At supper there were about ten of us left besides the Comissary. We were given sausage & coffee but no bread. I was sent up town to raise the bread. I went to the Committee of Safety who were going to give it to me, when two of the head comissary fellows came along. They began to growl at me & I hauled them over the coals in great shape. We got bread. After supper I walked 4 miles to Cooneville [Booneville], the next town where I slept.

MONDAY APR. 30 BOONEVILLE, COMMERCE VAL. JUNC. DES MOINES

I walked 15 miles into Des Moines, arriving in camp in time for supper. The Army is encamped at the stove works situated about a mile & a half east of the state capital. In Val Junction I met a detective belonging to my society. Also a fine lady. We all slept inside of the works. A great many intended to sleep by the fire but a fierce thunder storm arose & there was a grand scramble for shelter.

TUESDAY MAY 1 DES MOINES

Stayed in camp at the stove works, though the mayor has ordered us to move on. A perfect throng of visitors, fill the camp, while there are quite a lot of policemen on duty. In the afternoon the Salvation Army held services on the ground floor. Kelly, Baker, Speed & citizens spoke out side while the Des Moines boys & Soldier lads played ball. The Army won with a score of 27 to 19.

We spent the evening round the fire singing & joking till 11 when we went to bed. It was awful cold.

Wednesday was spent in camp. No Transportation.

Thursday the Des Moines Stars defeated the army's nine in a game of baseball with a score of 7 to 5.

Friday they were defeated by the Army boys with a score of 5 to 4.

Saturday morning we had two court martials. In the afternoon it was decided by the vote of the Army that we build flatboats, 150 in Number, to be 16 feet long & 6 wide. With these we are to go on down the Des Moines river to the Mississippi then on down to Cairo where we start up the Ohio to Wheeling W. Va. within 300 miles of our ultimate destination.

SUNDAY MAY 6.

Part of the Army went down to the Junction of the Coon &

Des Moines Rivers where by night fall 70 [or 75] boats were near finished.

Monday we worked all day & at night till 12.

Tuesday the stove works were abandoned & a camp established at the ship yards.

WEDNESDAY MAY 9.

We got under way, & ran down past & over a dam 2 miles to a bridge where we waited for orders, till 11:30, by which time over a hundred boats had passed us bound, God knows where. Then as no body appeared we got under way & by seven that night passed every boat & were the first to arrive at Runnels where about twenty of the foremost camped in the midst of a driving rain. We raised a few provisions & by 10:30 next morning after drying ourselves we got under way. We passed a few boats which had run by us & camped at Red Rock for the night. We are living without the comissary.

FRIDAY MAY 11.

Had an early breakfast & were soon passing boats. There were two 8 hours ahead which were impossible to overtake. Living fine. At 6 o'clock when 3 miles from Harvey where Col. Speed is stationed to stop lead boats, we were overtaken by a round bottomed boat manned by two Commissary bucks captained by the Captain of the day guards. They had orders to take possession of us but it was no go so they ordered us to wait for the main bunch while they proceeded to Harvey. I guess we will have to run past the town to night.

SATURDAY MAY 12.

After getting underway we soon found we were too lazy to paddle, so we drifted. As we reached Harvey the fleet overtook us, but bending to the paddles we soon left them tangled up & trying to run a dam. After awhile we went in swimming & when the boats over took us we pulled in to the bridge where provisions were to meet us. But by some mistake they were still at Oskaloosa a town of 16000 people 7 miles distant. Hundreds of teams were waiting

51   *The Tramp Diary*

to see us, & I guess on Sunday they went up into the thousands. From Des Moines & all along, the banks have been lined with the natives, & we would have to go for miles to find a secluded spot in which to bathe, or make our toilet. The boat containing our Capt. would not recognize us. And late that night when provisions arrived & the first meal for the majority of the boats was about to be cooked, we found we were not in it. The Liutenant with his boat took our part, & we cooked a pretty good meal out of our private commissary. We are going to hold an election to-morrow & as we are the majority we will oust the Captain.

SUNDAY MAY 13.

Held an election & the lieutenant was made captain. Then our two boats pulled across the river where we washed them out. Our old Captain went to Kelly & raised a roar & soon Kelly Speed & Baker came across & told us they were going to take our boat away & divide us into different companies, for our going ahead. We told them we would leave in a body & as all stood firm after a tally we were forgiven. So its all O.K.[25] At 1 P.M. we got underway and by evening arrived first boat at Eddyville. We held a vote & instead of sailing all night waited till morning when we pulled on empty stomachs. The rest of the boats have averaged one meal a day since leaving Desmoines & went one stretch of 48 hours.

MONDAY MAY 14.

As usual with our two boats lashed together we arrived first at Ottumwa & went over the dam on an improvised chute. We were taken a couple of miles below the town, which numbers 18000, to camp. That night the different boats started an opposition ferry & the cries of their rustlers reminded one of other days. We charged nothing, for payment was optional on their part.

TUESDAY. MAY 15

We were underway at 12 o'clock when the bugle sounded with three police boats & about 50 others ahead of us. We soon passed

---

[25]Joan London contends that the captain referred to here was Gorman and the lieutenant, H. R. Lytle, whose diary she relies on for details of these squabbles (p. 80).

them all but were stopped by the police boats & ordered astern. In a few minutes as we struck the bad part of the river, which extends 300 [30] or forty miles, the police boats ran aground, one after the other. We ran past, scraping the bars showing big rocks round which the water boiled & foamed, over others with such force as to almost stove us in till we were way ahead of the fleet which was tangled up & stranded in an astounding manner. We ran this 25 miles & then almost two more below the town of Eldon to camp. The rest of the boats soon began to string in, but by sun down they stopped arriving, & soon the news came that a couple of men had been hurt by Pinkertons at the bridge and all boats were stopping. Two of the detectives were arrested but the R.R. officials instantly bailed them out. By nine o'clock the boats came in all in a lump, & they were all greatly excited. If any Pinkertons are captured Woe unto them for the men are getting desperate.

WEDNESDAY. MAY 16.

Early in the morning one of our boats crossed the river but 25 Pinkertons refused them landing. In an instant every boat was full of excited men crossing the river, while others disdaining such slow traveling were wading the ford never stopping to even pull off their shoes & stocks or roll up their pants. When the P's saw this wild array approaching they all took to their heels but two who maintained their ground. But they were surrounded, & the jam saved them to a great extent though they were still severely punished, & their pistols taken away. By that time Kelly gained control of his men, & they returned to camp for breakfast while he gave the P's good talking to. We left at 12 with Col. Speed aboard & passing every boat were soon in the lead. Col. Baker overtook us in a buggy & came aboard. The Omaha Bee, & 9 others of Co K's boats lashed together gave us a hard pull but strength & endurance won the day & when we camped alongside the bridge at Pittsburg they were out of sight. The army could not overtake & but 5 boats camped with us.

THURSDAY MAY 17.

We started early but the army had already passed. By the time we reached Keosochwa [Keosauqua] we had overtaken them, & running the rapids with safety found half a dozen stove in & on the beach getting repaired while the pop corn man lost five hundred cigars & swamped his boat with wife child & entire outfit on board. We received our morning rations & with a fair wind soon passed the fleet. They are getting tired but once in a while some crack crew gives us a spin to their disgust & our delight. We were the first to go over the dam on a chute prepared by the citizen's of Bonaparte. We then went into camp.

FRIDAY MAY 18.

We passed a miserable day on the water with a chilling wind & driving rain. In the after noon we camped in Missouri where we passed a miserable night

SATURDAY MAY 19.

Pulled out without breakfast with Col. Speed aboard. With sail & oar we passed Genl. Kelly & then Col. Baker & were the first in to the bridge a mile & a half from Keoukuk [Keokuk]. Are all busy lashing the boats together into a raft.

SUNDAY MAY 20.

The raft was completed but the wind was to high to venture out on the Mississippi. We had a slim breakfast at six & that lasted all day.

We pulled out Monday May 21 & arrived at Quincy at 2 P.M. covering a distance of 40 miles. We had nothing to eat from six the day before till five to day.

TUESDAY MAY 22.

We changed our camp to Goose Island.

Wednesday in camp, busy decking the boats in groups of fours.

THURSDAY MAY 24.

Left Quincy at 4:30 P.M. & floated down to Hannibal Mo. a distance of 22 miles, arriving at 10. We had quite a time in finding our camp on an Is. on the Ill. side. We went supperless to bed. Am going to pull out in the morning. I can't stand starvation.

FRIDAY MAY 25.

Charley Veiting, known as the "boiler maker" & I left the camp on the island. We went ashore on the Ill. side in a skiff, & walked six miles on the C. B. & Q. to Fell Creek. We had gone six miles out of our way. But we got on a hand car & rode six miles to Hulls, on the Wabash. While there we met McAvoy, Fish, Scotty, & Davy who had also quit the army.

SATURDAY MAY 26.

At 2:11 A.M. we caught the "Cannon ball. as she slowed up at the crossing. Scotty & Davy, who is sick, were ditched. The four of us were ditched at the Bluffs. 40 miles farther. In the afternoon Fish & McAvoy caught a freight while Charley & I were away eating dinner.

SUNDAY MAY 27.

At 3:21 A.M. We caught the "Cannon ball" & found Scotty & Davey on the blind. We were all ditched at daylight at Jacksonville. The C. & A. runs through here & we are going to take that. Charley went off, but didnot return. Guess he caught a train.

MONDAY MAY 28.

Charley did not return. Scotty & Davey went off to sleep somewhere & did not return in time to catch the K.C. Passenger at 3:30. I caught her & rode her till after sun rise to Mason City. 25000 inhabitants, 45 miles from Jacksonville. Caught a cattle train & rode all night.

TUESDAY MAY 29.

Arrived in Chicago at 7 A.M. Strolled down to the Post Office & found 9 letters, one registered awaiting me. Received $4 in Greenbacks.[26] After mailing a letter I went down amongest the Jews of South Clark st. where after a great deal of wrangling & talking I bought shoes, overcoat, hat, pants & shirt. Then with a shave & a good dinner I started out to see the sights. Went to the

---

[26]At this point in her two-volume biography, Charmian London prints the earliest known letter (dated May 22, 1894) to London from his mother and which he probably received in Chicago (*The Book of Jack London,* I, pp. 160-161).

theater in the evening, & then to bed. The first bed I had lain in since leaving home.

WEDNESDAY MAY 30. DECORATION DAY

I spent the better part of the day at the World's Fair grounds. In the evening went to the Salvation Army & then to another 15 cent Bed.

THURSDAY MAY 31.

Went out in the morning to Lincoln Park & at 12 took the steamer City of Chicago for St. Joseph, Mich. It is a 60 mile run across Lake Michigan. I found Aunt Mary lived a mile & a half from town, but I was soon there receiving a hearty welcome.

KELLEY'S ARMY[27]

Character Studies.

Stew. His manner of beating trains. Sleeping with one eye open. How he missed the Industrial Army, & lost his stew at Roseville Junction.

The English Lad.

How he had the giggles. How he worked in the restaurant at Truckee chasing chickens in the yard & only catching one. Swipe 6 tenderloin stakes & his pockets full of potatoes. Rolling cigars for all hands.

The Irish boy from Dublin. His good advice & evil tendencies.
The long lean Yankee from Cairo. "May as well have the game as the name." If the old folks would only know how to treat a fellow when he comes home & not give him any guff it would be all right." Going home to feed up, pass the winter & be in good condition for next summer.

The Irishman in Terrace & his intelligence & travels.

The lad from Minneapolis Minnesota, & his postal order.

The swede from Chicago.

The Turk & the Greek.

INCIDENTS & ADVENTURES[28]

The brakeman coming over the Hill. "Dig up" Dig up" How much stuff have you got. Dig up." No I wouldnot take a man's last cent. If I take your tobacco what are you going to do?

---

[27]"Kelly's Army" appears first in the tramp diary — before any of the daily entries. The last four items seem to have been added at another time.

[28]"Incidents & Adventures" comes between the entries for May 18 and May 19 and takes up five pages in the diary. Several of these episodes are used in *The Road*.

No. What not even the price of the whiskey. Well seeing as you fellows aint going to treat I'll have to do it my self. Produces bottle, & drinks while "the jeweler" holds the lantern on high. Then treats all hands to a swig except Stew who only gets a smell of the cork. Gives us warning & tips as to our line of action at the different stations. Bids us good bye just before entering the snow-sheds.

How we got ditched at Truckee.

Falling asleep in the chairs at the Hotel & getting the bounce.

The burning overcoat & flying cinders as I was crossing the desert on a through freight going fifty miles an hour.

Breaking & passing coal for a division.

The great preponderance of Swedes & Germans.

Honesty of a great majority of hobos, & good heartedness. Good Counsel. The majority willing & eager for work. Gathering in groups & discussing the chances in different parts of the country.

The depot deserted during the day. Only perhaps a couple of hobos to be seen. As the shades of night draw on they begin to issue from their retreats & soon there is a crowd congregated of from 12 or 15 to 50.

Sleeping in the round house by the stove. An everchanging crowd. Coming & going as every train pulls in or out.

Sleeping in the Electric Light Works in Evanston. The horrible heat. My restlessness. Searching for water. Kindly directed to go down through the snow to the river. Sitting in the snow till I froze then back to the boilers where I baked.

The two cattle punchers. Long & Shorty & their carouse in Rock Springs. Scraps & drinks between.

The red hot cinder striking in the hollow of the neck. Acting like a madman.

The difference of speed on the road. The quiet easy going, the slow pokes & the comets. Strange meetings, by series of accident & ditches an easy goer overtakes a comet but is left in the end. The ease the kids have in beating their way. Good crews & bad crews. Sometimes met in streaks.

The Kangaroo Court. With 50 & 25 cops. Recreation Song or dance the Judge

Grumbling before dinner, happy after dinner.

Breaking camp in Van Meter in the midst of the thunder storm. Storming the comissary next morning.

S.P.	Southern Pacific[29]
C.P.	Central Pacific
U.P.	Union Pacific
U.T.L.	Union Tank Line
C.F.T.	California Fruit Transportation
C.F.X.	California Fruit Express

---

[29]The names of these railroads appear after the final entries (May 30-31) in the diary.

stiff.[30]
push.
batter.
set down
hand out
poke out
privates
mooching
kip
shiv.
floater.
chuck
smondge [?]
scoffs

Java
Jerry house
Jerry gang
wipe
floppins
mulligan.
rollin a stiff
Alke stiff
Alke gang
lum.
light piece
dynamiter. [dynaniter ?]
glam.
swiped. [sniped?]

---

[30]This list of tramp terms follows the page of railroad names, and the first entries (April 6-7) commence after this page.

"'Frisco Kid's Story"

London tried to sell his first two tramp sketches to other magazines after their initial appearance in The Aegis. *Parts of the Frisco Kid stories are utilized in Chapters XVI-VII of* The Cruise of the Dazzler *(1902). In fact, London first titled the book "'Frisco Kid," but the character carrying this name is a sailor and not a road kid. James E. Sisson points out that in these sketches the Frisco Kid foreshadows the remarkable figure of the Malemute Kid, who appears in London's early Klondike stories: Sisson, ed., "Jack London's Articles and Short Stories in* The (Oakland) High School Aegis," *The London Collector, III (December 1971), 1-7. A brief notebook titled "Magazine Sales #1" (on deposit with an uncatalogued addendum to the JLP, HEH) includes dates of London's attempts to sell the "Frisco Kid" sections of* The Cruise of the Dazzler.

Who am I? Why I'm de "Frisco Kid." An' wot do I do? I'm on de "road," see! Say, youze ain't got nothin' agin me, have yer, mister? Cos if yer has, I'll chase meself off, fer I'm pretty good at pacin'. No, you hasn't? Well, den I guess it's all square. Yer see I took yer fer a fly cop, an' I'm onto meself fer a jigger w'en it comes to dem people.

Wot! A quarter? Dat's very kind in yer, mister. Now I'se solid fer me bed an' a bowl of Java in de mornin'. Yer wants ter ast me a few questions? Den fire away. I'se yer red hot tomale.

A kid wid curley golden hair an fair complexshun, an' 'bout des size of me? Well, I guess I seed stacks like'm, but I never took pertic'lar notiss, dough if I spots'm I'll put yer on. W'en did he

Source: *The High School Aegis,* X (February 15, 1895), 2-3; (November 4 1895), 2-4.

stray away, an' wot's his monica? I mean wot's his name? Yer see we all travels by monicas on de road. Charley wuz his handle? Say! did he wear his hair middlin' long like a girl's, an' hail from Frisco? Den I guess I knowed'm onst. Say! if I tells yer all I knows about'm, yer won't give me de cross hop, will yer? Didn't he sport a little hoop — Hoop? — O' I see yer a gentleman, an' don't talk like me and de people I travel wid. I mean a ring, a gold un, set wid little, red rubies? — I guess dat's wot yer calls'm. An' a locket? Yes, I knows de locket too. It opens an' shuts, an' dere's a little pitcher of a lady on one side an' some hair, yaller hair like his, only different, on de other. Do I know w'ere dey is? Yer jest bet I do — here dey is. I allus wore dem roun' my neck since he ———— Say! Leave go! Don't squeeze me arm like dat. Yer hurts, yer do, an' wot der yer tink I am? A cheap guy?

Yer wants ter know w'ere he is? Den jes' take it easy, an' don't get leary and grab me like dat again, an' I'll tell yer all I knows.

Yer see it wuz dis way. Las' year 'bout dis time, me'en and my pal, "Leary Joe" come down to Sacramento to work de fair. Well, one hot day — an' it wuz a scorcher — Leary Joe got to sloppin' up on white line, an wuz orioide. Den I takes'm to bed, an' not knowin' wot to do wid meself, took a stroll. I wuz mopin' down de main drag, I mean de main street, w'en I bumped up gainst de kid wid de yaller hair. He was wid four er five hobos, an' w'en I seed his good togs, an' hoop an' gold ticker, I tumbled to wot de gang wuz up to. So I t'ought I'd snare'm meself, an' I up an' sez, jest like we wuz ol' fren's, "Say, kid, w'ere yer ben all day? Come on; let's go swimmin'." Yer see, I tought I'd like ter get a finger in de pie meself.

I guess he didn't kinder like de tuff looks of de crowd, an' de swimmin' got his eye, so he gives de push de shake and does de swift sneak. An' yer ough'to seen de gang. Dey'd liked ter a chewed me up an' pushed me nose in, only dey dassant, cos dey wer' fraid of me pal, Leary Joe, fer he wuz de swiftest scrapper on de drag.

Well, we went swimmin'. On de way I found dat de kid'd run away from home an' jest hit de road. So I ast 'm if he wanted ter travel wid me an' my pal Leary Joe, cos if he did, we were willin', an' he said "Yes." Somehow, I cudn't tell why, I kinder took ter dat kid. He wus so pritty an' innisent like, jest as if he wuz a girl. An' if I cussed, he'd kinder blush an' wudn't look at me fer a long while. An' den I tumbled dat he had good people an' wuzn't ust to swearin'. An' jest like yer, he wuz allus callin' me down, cos he didn't understand de words I talked, an' den I'd cut de rag short an' tell 'm wot dey ment. But he wuz smart, I tell yer; yer didn't have ter give 'm de drop more'n onst to make 'm tumble.

Well, we moped up above de railroad bridge an' undrest on a san'bar w'ere a lot other road-kids, wot I knowed, wuz in swimmin'. Say! it wuz a sight ter see dat yaller-haired kid's clo's. Right down ter de skin dey wuz as fine as fine cud be. A good 'eal better'n I ever wore.

At first, de road-kids wuz fer guyin' 'm, but I bluff 'm wid der stiff lip, an' dey let up an' wuz very kind ter 'm. It wuz a picnic ter see dat kid. He wuz so funny an' diffrent from de rest of de push. He wuz so innisent an' trustin' like. Why, he guv me his hoop ter wear fer 'm, cos he wuz leary dat it'd slip off'n his finger in de water. An' w'en he took his locket off'n his neck an' put it in his pocket, curius like, I took it ter see wot it wuz like, an' if it wuz snide. But it wuz eighteen K., an' den I kep' it, so de odder kids cudn't swipe it.

Well, we had lots of joy, an' so did de kid, dough he couldn't swim a stroke. Bime'by we all cum out an' lay on de sand in de sun 'cept 'm, an' he staid in, foolin' 'round in de shaller places. Pritty quick I got ter jokin' wid 'm, an' I can see 'm now wid his han's claspt behind his head, an' his pritty face all smiles an' laffin', an' his yaller hair flyin' ev'ry way, like a girl's. He wuz walkin' out backwards from de san'bar.

All of a sudden like, he struck a hole an' went down. We wuz all in de water like a shot, but he never cum up any more. Yer see, he struck de undertow an' wuz sucked down. Well, bime'by we all got out an' sat in der san' kinder solem' like fer a long while. Yer see, it wuz hard ter see a poor innisent kid like dat get drownded, even dough we hadn't knowed 'm very long.

Pritty soon, after a while, de "Punk Kid" goes up an' takes de ticker, I mean watch, sayin' fer an excuse like, "Mine's broke." But he didn't need ter 'polygize, fer up goes de "Miget Kid" an' take his coat, an' de "Cookey Kid" his shirt, an' so on, till dere wuz nothin' left but his kicks, I mean shoes, w'ich I took, coz mine wuz no good. Den we piles up our ole rags in place of his good 'uns, an' drest.

De "Orator Kid" went an' gave de coroner de tip, an' den run out of de office, so dey cudn't pinch 'm. An' w'en de coroner cum down, all drest up fine, an' took de clo's, he said kinder offhand like, w'en he saw de poor, mis'rable rags: "It's only a tramp kid, anyhow."

Well' t'ree days went by, an' den dey foun' de poor little kid way down de river, an' w'en he wuz at de morgue, I went an' took a look at 'm.

Wot? Yer say, why didn't I 'dentify 'm? Well, yer see it wuz dis way: "Leary Joe" an' me wuz goin' ter pull out nex' day, an' I didn't wanter be held fer de inquest, an' besides, dey might ast me some curius questions 'bout wot became of his good togs and jewelery.

Wot? Yu're not cryin', are yer mister? Well, yu're de funniest guy I ever seen. O! I tumbles now. Yer wuz de kid's ole man. Den I'm sorry fer yer, an' here's my hand on it.

Wot? Five big cart-wheels! I'm much obliged, mister, an' I guess yu'd better keep de hoop an' locket, cos dey belongs ter yer anyways. Well, I must be sayin' "So long," cos here cums my pal Leary Joe, an' we're goin' out on dat freight over dere. Dere she whistles now, an' I must be movin'. Cum on, Leary Joe, an' take de second, she's nice an' clean, an' we can have a good snooze.

"And 'Frisco Kid Came Back"

"Hello ye stiffs! — got the makin's? I got ter smoke so bad I can taste it. Say! its like t'ree squares a day an' a hold me down, ter be wid yer onst more.

"Wot'v I been doin' wid meself? an, w'ere did I snare me good togs? Well, it's dis way. I wuz down in me luck — way down in G — way down under me uppers — Say! I wuz down dat far I fell clear troo' an' cum up on top on de udder side — way up in C. Say! yer wudn't a knowed me!

"Dis is how de presto change happened. I struck a jay town on de C. B. and Q. jerk an' got hoodooed. I battered a house fer me breakfas' an' bumpt up inter a red-headed woman. Say! I wuz dat rattled I fergot ter steal de soap. De nex' house I slammed de gate at, dere wuz a cross-eyed man, an' I didn't spit in me hat. Dat done me all up. I was clean off me nut wid de hoodoo.

"After dat I cudn't put me han' ter nuthin' widout gettin' de gee hee. Nuthin' went O. K. Bimeby, w'en I wuz mopin' up de main-drag, I struck a guy fer de price, an' he wuz a fly cop an, I got thirty days. Dat settled me. Me name wuz Mud. I wuz not in it. I wuz outen de movement.

"W'en I did me time I wuz goin' ter give de burg de swift an' elegant side sneak — but I didn't. An' dats how I fell clean troo'. Dere wuzn't a freight along 'till dark, so I chases meself around ter have a swim. Den I swiped a kid's line an' went ter fishin'. Dey wudn't bite. I cudn't ketch a cat. I cudn't ketch nuthin' 'till an old Rube take a tumble to himself offen de end. He cum sailin' by wid a horrible thirst on — he cudn't get enuff. I trowed 'm de line an' snared 'm de firs' rattle outen de box.

"W'en I got 'm landed, he sez, 'Yer me saviour.'

" 'So yer tellin' me,' sez I.

" 'Yer an angel,' sez he.

" 'Yer bet yer sweet life,' sez I.

" 'I'll reward ye,' sez he.

" 'Now yer shoutin',' sez I.

"Say! dat old guy chases me home, an' after he chewed de rag wid his ole woman — mebbe yer tinkin' I'm tellin' yer a fairy story — but may I never get de price again, if dey didn't adopt me.

"I tole dem me tale of woe. Wot did I w'isper? I tole 'm how me ole man uster t'ump me ole woman w'en he got an edge on, an' I tole 'm how pious she wuz, an' how she uster tell me to be upright an' noble — an' how she kicked de bucket wid a broken heart, an' how de ole man kicked me out, an' how he swilled like 'r fish till he kicked de pig, too. Me little song wuz nuthin' but kick — 'fer tell yer de truth,' sez I, 'I wuz never growed up, I wuz kicked up. Dat's how I cum here — I wuz kicked here.'

"Den de o'e girl took me in her arms an' sez, 'Me poor boy.' An' de ole boy blows his bandana fit ter kill, an' I makes de stage hit by cryin' meself. Say! dat brung down de house — we all blubbered.

"De old girl — say! she was a nice ole girl! — she sez I wud never get kicked no more, an' de ole hoss, he sez he had enuff fer ter take care 'v me too. Dat's how I fell troo' me luck an' cum out on top.

"W'y didn't I hol' it down? Wot are yer givin' us? Wait till I give yer me spiel. It was no snap, see! Dey wuz too good fer me. Every mornin' de ole man 'ud read a chapter from de book, an' every time I'd get settled down ter tinkin' 'v de gang, he'd ask me wot de las' verse wuz, an' w'en I didn't know, he'd look dat hurt it 'd make me feel bad. I never cud listen, 'cept w'en he'd read about Joshua. Say! he wuz a scrapper fer yer life! Den I liked Samson, too. De barbers were on a strike w'ere he lived, an' he wuz stronger dan a locomotive. Parts wuz as good as Deadwood Dick an Nick Carter, an' w'en he cum to w'ere an ole bloke wuz dat long winded, he lived over nine hundred years. Say! it wuz out uv sight; but den dey wuz a whole lot 'v dem an' I got weary. An' w'en he'd read about dere sons, an' de sons of dem sons, an' de sons of dem sons, an' all de udder sons beside, I'd pound me ear an' snore.

"Den, I cudn't quit swearin', an' every time I'd rip a big 'n out, de old gal 'd show de whites 'v her eyes an' say, "Thomas!" long an' solemn' an' reprovin' like.

"An' dey wud allus smell me breath ter see if I'd ben smokin'. An' dey wudn't let me eat wid me knife, nor spill de Java out 'n me saucer. I cudn't never ketch on ter dere style. I was allus jabbin' me knife inter de butter dish, or fergettin' ter put de sugar spoon back in de bowl. Den I chewed out loud an' dat scraped on dere nerves. An' I'd allus fergit an' put de napkins in me pocket w'en I wuz done. Den dey made me sport me head piece straight on me nut, an' dey sed I swung me shoulders too much w'en I walked.

"Den I kep' gettin' inter scraps wid de kids on de block. Had to do somethin' fer excitement, see! One time I got a lot 'v dem on de back fence, an' made 'm sit in a row, wid each a chew of Star in his han'. W'en I guv de word dey all began ter chew. De kid dat chewed de longes' wuz ter get a bird uv a kite I made fer de occasion. Say! yer outen seen dem kids. W'en I called time, dere wuzn't one left on de fence. Yer'd t'ink de cholera 'd struck de town de way dey all chased home, sick. Say! yer outen ben dere. Dere mudders waltzed over ter de house in flocks an' pestered de life outen de ole girl. Dey sed I wuz corruptin' de good morals uv dere sons, an' dat I was a menace ter dere lives an' property.

"I got inter lots uv scrapes like dat; but I allus jollied dem up an' made it all right. Dey tried ter sen' me ter school — Say! I got de G. B. de firs' day. Dey never got tired — dey wuz allus tryin' ter improve me. Dey wuz bound ter make a good boy outen me, an' I wuz boun' dey wudn't.

"Bimeby I got homesick. I got ter t'inking of de road again — of de gang an 'de good ole times I had wid dem. Say! it 'd make me heart jump w'en I'd hear an engine whistle, an' I'd t'ink 'v freights an' passengers, an' remember how I uster ketch de blind an' shinny up ter de decks, or grab a gunnel an' swing underneath. An' I wuz jes' dyin' fer a game uv craps 'r seven up. I made up me mind dat de adoption scheme was N. G. One day I got ter rememberin' de las' mulligan I had. Yer knows de time — w'en Pittsburg Joe bummed de butcher-shops, an' Chi Slim de bakeries, an' de Montana Sports de groceries, an' you an' I swiped de chickens, w'ile Moulder Blackey got de beer, an' Leary Joe made de fire, an' Skysail Jack did de cookin'. Say! it made me mouth water ter t'ink uv it. I cudn't stand it no longer, so I guv me adopted parents de ditch, an' hit de road onst more.

"Ah! dere's de greasy, ole deck again. Don't care 'f I do. I'll go yer jes' onst fer luck. Cut fer deal — Jack High."

"The Road"

This essay was first submitted in 1897 for publication in the San Francisco Examiner. *That newspaper and at least three others rejected the article before the* Arena *accepted it in 1899. London was so certain of its publication in the summer of 1899 that he told a newspaper reporter of his success, and he wrote a friend about its appearance; but the essay was returned in March of 1900 "as unavailable under amended policy of new owners." The article remained unpublished until it appeared in* Jack London Reports *(1970). See the editor's headnote to the story on p. 311. No. 1: Magazine Sales. From 1898 to May 1900," Box 19, JCLC, USU; "An Oakland Boy's Success as a Story Writer," unidentified clipping dated November 22, 1899, Jack London Scrapbooks 1, p. 7, JLP, HEH;* Letters, *pp. 45, 50.*

The "Road," the hog-train, or for brevity's sake, the hog: It is a realm almost as unexplored as fairyland, yet hardly as impregnable. Nay, in fact, destiny not only entices but forces world-weary mortals into its embrace. It entices romantic and unruly boys, who venture along its dangerous ways in search of fortune or in rash attempt to escape parental discipline. It seizes with relentless grip the unfortunate who drifts with, or struggles against the tide of human affairs. Those who cannot go whither must come thither, all hope behind. It is the river of oblivion, of which the soul-wanderer, shuddering with coward's heart (or religious scruple at self destruction, must drink. Henceforth all

Source: *Jack London Reports: War Correspondence, Sports Articles, and Miscellaneous Writings*, edited by King Hendricks and Irving Shepard. Garden City, New York: Doubleday and Company, 1970, pp. 311-321.

identity is lost. Though with many aliases, not even the semi-respectable number of the convict is his. He has but one designation; they all have it: — Tramp. But the law aids him, however, if reputation grows with syllables, for under it he is known as vagrant. Yet herein is a double injustice done. While all tramps are vagrant, all vagrants are not tramps: Many are worse, a thousand times worse than the tramp. And again, the small bit of respectability which may yet linger about his former name is destroyed. He is a vagrant: It is shortened to "Vag." Three letters, two consonants and a vowel, stand between him and the negation of being. He is on the ragged edge of nonentity.

We all know the tramp — that is, we have seen him and talked with him. And what an eyesore he has always been! Perhaps, when hurrying home through the rainy night, all comfortable in mackintosh, umbrella and overshoes, he has dawned upon us like a comet, malignant of aspect. Wet, shivering, and miserable, whining for the price of a bed or a meal, he casts his baleful influence over us: Nor can hastily given largesse or abrupt refusal overcome it. Our comfort seems out of place, actually jars upon us. We are thrown out of our good humor and rudely awakened from the anticipatory dream we have dreamed all day at the office — the snug little home, all cheery, bright and warm; the smiling wife and her affectionate greeting; the laughing children, or perhaps the one little crowing tot, the son and heir. We have met him [the tramp] in the park, always occupying the best benches; on the overland and summer excursions; at the springs and at the seaside: In short, we have met him everywhere, even desecrating the sanctity of our back stoop, where he ate of the crumbs of our table. Still, his land is an unknown region, and we are less conversant with his habits and thoughts than with those of the inhabitants of the Cannibal Islands.

One astonishing thing about Trampland is its population. Variously estimated by equally competent authorities at from 500,000 to 1,500,000 it will be found that 1,000,000 is not far out of the way. A million! It seems impossible, yet is a fact. If a Stanley may be lost in Africa, cannot such a number be lost in the United States? This is rendered easy because of the breadth of country and the evenness of their distribution. Every town, village, railroad station, watering-tank and siding, has its proportion; in the great metropolises their numbers mount into the tens of thousands; while each county and city jail has its due quota, supported by the taxpayer. It is only when concentrated that their abundance is manifested. One example will suffice. On a rainy morning in the spring of '94, an army of then, 2,000 strong, marched out of Council Bluffs. They had, as an organization, already traveled two thousand miles and their numbers were augmenting at every step. At their head rode their leader on a handsome black charger, presented him by an enthusiastic farmer. They were marshalled in divisions and companies and had staff officers, couriers, aid-de-campes [sic], buglers, banner-bearers, army physicians and fully equipped medical department, a fife and drum corps, a healthy strong-box, and efficient police service, a commissary, and above all, the best of discipline. The stationary Negro population is often called the incubus of the South; but is not this increasing, shifting, tramp population, not passive like the Negro but full of the indomitability of the Teuton, equally worthy of consideration, and by the whole race?

Strange as it may seem, in this outcast world the sharp lines of caste are as rigorously drawn as in the world from which it has evolved. There are several prominent divisions. The Simon-pure tramp, hence professional, calls himself "The Profesh." He is not the one we meet with so profusely in *Judge* or *Puck*. The only resemblance lies in that he never works. He does not carry a tomato-can on a string, wear long hair, or manifest his calling in his dress. His clothes are almost always good, never threadbare, torn, and dirty. In fact, with him, the comb, cake of soap, looking-glass and clothes brush are indispensables. He lives better and more easily than the average workingman. Having reduced begging to a fine art, he scorns back stoops and kitchen tables, patronizes the restaurant, and always has the price of the drinks about him. His is the class most to be feared. Many of them have "done time" and are capable and worthy of doing more. They will commit, under stress of circumstance and favorable opportunity, every crime on the calendar, and then, just a few more besides. Perhaps the simile is unjust, but they are looked up to as the aristocracy of their underworld.

The largest class is that of the working tramp. That is, the tramp who looks for work and is not afraid of it when he finds it. He usually carries his blankets and is somewhat akin to his more respectable Australian compatriot, who strikes off into the "bush" with his "swag" and "billy-can." Because of his predilection to carrying his bed with him, he is known in trampland as the "bindle stiff." The etymology of this phrase is simple: Any tramp is a "stiff," and the blanket in a bundle is a "bindle." These are the men, who, in New York, travel into the Genesee country to the hops; in the Dakotas, to the harvests; in Michigan, to the berry-picking; and in California, to the vintage, hops and harvest.

The "Stew Bum" is the most despised of his kind. He is the *Canaille,* the *Sansculotte,* the fourth estate of trampland. Of such stuff are squawmen made. It is he who is the prototype of the individual aforementioned, who graces the pages of our humorous periodicals. He is not supremely wicked nor degraded: deep-sunk in a state of languorous lassitude, he passively exists, viewing the active world with philosophic soul. His one ambition, one dream, one ideal is stew: Hence his only evil trait — an electric affinity which always draws him and chicken roosts into close conjunction.

A curious class, closely connected in career with the China-town bum who drinks cheap gin and fills an early grave, is that of the "Alki Stiffs." "Alki" is the argot for alcohol. They travel in gangs and are a close approach to communists, only differing in that they have no community of goods. The reason for this is simple: They have no goods. But the ideal commune could not vie with them in a community of drink. Every penny, begged or stolen, goes to the purchase of their fiery beverage, of which all may drink. The finest mixer of the "cocktail route" cannot approach them in the art of diluting alcohol with water. Too much water and it is spoiled: Too little, and they are spoiled, for then and there is much devastation done to the linings of their stomachs. Masters there are among them, but they have seldom served a long apprenticeship:

Death comes too soon for that. In the world, when a man falls, he takes to drink: In trampland, to the "white line," as they tritely call it. Somehow, one never meets a gang of these poor devils lying in the grass and wild flowers of the country wayside, sleeping and drowsing in the depths of debauch, without being reminded of Tennyson's *Lotus Eaters,* who swore and kept an oath: —

In the hollow lotus-land to live and lie reclined
On the hills like gods together, careless of mankind.

The cripples, usually traveling in pairs, often are to be met with in gangs of twenty or more. A universal custom with such groups is to have two or three of the most brutal of the "profesh" as body guard. These fight their battles, run their errands, handle their money, and take care of them when they are drunk. In return, these mercenaries are given their meal and drink money. It is amusing to witness the meeting of two stranger cripples. Each will solicitously enquire as to how the other lost his limb. Then will follow a detailed account of its amputation, with criticism of the surgeons who officiated and their methods, the conversation usually terminating with an adjournment to some secluded spot, where, with all the fondness of paternal affection, they compare stumps. One touch of amputation makes all cripples kin.

Then there is a transient class, a sort of general miscellany, composed of all kinds of men temporarily down in their luck. Among these, the most interesting character studies may be made. Strikingly diverse and powerful individualities are here found, all bound in a mesh of pathos and ludicrity [sic]. Most of them are men whose money has given out and who are forced to make their way home as best they can. Farmer boys, turning their backs on the city; city-bred men, turning away from the country; men who have been fleeced and are too proud to write or wire for help; others, fleeing from justice; some who have been indiscreet; many who have tried to cut too brilliant a dash; broken down actors, sports and tinhorns; and even some (a small percentage) who, parsimoniously inclined, wish to save their railroad fare. Nearly all of them are possessed of a little money and furnish rich plucking to mean railroad men and the "profesh." They are to be known at a glance. Their ignorance of the customs and unwritten rules of the "road" paint their greenness as vividly as does the unsophistication and lack of conventionality of our friend the "hayseed," when he comes to town. They are wanderers in a strange land and the scrapes and pitfalls they stumble into, are laughable yet often tragic.

Another division, which is merely a sub-class and closely allied to the "profesh," is that of the "Fakirs." There are tinkers, umbrella menders, locksmiths, tattooers, tooth-pullers, quack doctors, corn doctors, horse doctors — in short, a lengthy list. Some sell trinkets and gew gaws and others, "fakes." These "fakes" are as curious and interesting as they are innumerable. We all remember the Frenchman who made flea powder out of pulverized brick — this is the nature of the "fake." Here is a sample, as simple as it is successful: — The prudent housewife meets at the door a glib young individual, who shows her a piece of tin, so closely perforated with tiny holes that it is almost a gauze. He gives a rambling a [sic] very impressive disquisition on the principles of the kerosene lamp, then explains that this tin, fitted to the top of the wick, will give twice the flame, burn less oil, and never burn the wick which will thus last forever. He even volunteers to attach it to her oldest lamp and if she be not convinced it costs her nothing; if convinced, only fifteen cents. She brings from some top shelf an old lamp, long since fallen into disuse. Very business-like, he produces pinchers and snippers and sets to work, volubly chattering all the while. Examining the ancient burner and deftly opening the clogged flues and air vents, he attaches his tin. Then he lights it and the admiring housewife beholds a flame, larger and more luminous than that of her best parlor lamp. After receiving his fifteen cents, he advises her to give it a trial for that night and promises to call next day. He duplicates this operation in the whole neighborhood. In the evening, the wondrous flame is the center of interest in the family circle — "So saving! And so cheap! Father, we must have them on all the lamps." Next day the young man reappears and puts his little "fake" on every burner in the house. He receives anywhere from fifty cents to a dollar for a couple of cents worth of low grade tin, and vanishes for ever, as Carlyle would say, "Into outer darkness." But O, 'tis passing fair! Two days suffice: The tin drops off.

Saddest of all, is the training school of the "Road." Man, vicious and corrupt, the incarnation of all that is vile and loathsome, is a melancholy object; but how much more, is innocent youth, rapidly becoming so! Modification by environment — O pregnant term! In it lies all the misery and all the joy of mankind, all the purest and all the most degraded soul-developments, all the noblest and foulest attributes and deeds. Man, blindly-groping, with weak, finite conception, personifies these antitheses in the powers of light and darkness: Yet, even to man, poor earthworm, is given the power to qualify these personifications of his, through *modification by environment*. Still, we, Americans, and partakers of the science and culture of our tremendous civilization, cognizant of all this, allow in our midst the annual prostitution of tens of thousands of souls. Boy tramps or "Road-kids" abound in our land. They are children, embryonic souls — the most plastic of fabrics. Flung into existence, ready to tear aside the veil of the future; with the mighty pulse of dawning twentieth century throbbing about him; with the culminated forces of the thousand dead and the one living civilization effervescing in the huge world-caldron, they are cast out, by the cruel society which gave them birth, into a nether world of outlawry and darkness.

But to the "Road-kids." Many are run-aways, who, through romantic dreaming or undue harshness, have left comfortable homes for the stern vicissitudes of tramp life. The romantic always return, but of those who have been cruelly treated, virtually none. These cases may be sad, but there is still a second division — the children, begotten of ignorance, poverty and sin. Uncultivated, with no helping hand to guide their faltering footsteps, with the brand of Cain upon their brows, they raise their moan in silent brute-anguish to a cold world and drift into trampland, the scape-goats of their generation. To become what? "Alki Stiffs" and "Stew Bums"? Perhaps; but almost always to become of the "Profesh" the most professional. Inscrutable scheme of life! Cast out and scourged by society, their mother, they return, the scourge of their mother, society. We have all wept for little Oliver Twist; nor have we failed to reserve a copious draught for Nancy Stykes [sic] — she was a woman; but the artful dodger, who weeps for him? Yet his is the saddest of all.

Though sometimes journeying in gangs, they often travel with members of the "Profesh." A gang of them, composed of the more intrepid and vicious, is a terrible thing to meet. They are wolves in human guise. Besides committing all sorts of sly and petty depredations, they hunt higher game. "Rolling a stiff," as they call robbing a drunken man, is a mere pastime; but they do not refrain from attacking sober ones. Like wolves, they fly at the throat, giving what is known as the "strong arm." This is applied from behind, the large bone of the wrist and the victim's windpipe coming into painful and dangerous juxtaposition. Those who travel with the "Profesh" are serving their criminal apprenticeship. They are very useful, and in some crimes even indispensable. It is a hard school and they learn rapidly, soon finding the proper field for the exercise of their peculiar talents. The faithfulness of the "Road-kids" for their teachers or "pals" and vice versa, is often pathetic. The self-sacrifice, hardship and punishment they will undergo for each other, is astonishing — a sure index to the latent nobility of soul which lurks within, dwarfed instead of developed. Poor devils! With the hand of society raised against them, it is the only opening through which the shrunken higher parts of their nature may be manifested.

Clothing, eating, and sleeping are not so difficult to obtain in trampland; but of the three, a comfortable place to sleep is the hardest. In the cities and large towns, a goodly portion buy their meals with money begged on the street. Others, not so bold, go from house to house, "slamming gates," as they picturesquely describe it. When at a back door, eatables are given them wrapped in paper, they call it a "poke-out" or "hand-out." This is not prized so highly as a "set-down" (going into the kitchen). Above all the tramp likes his "java" (coffee). Especially in the morning after a cold night, they, all-benumbed, prefer it to all the "hand-outs" in

Christendom. As to clothes: Some, being lazy, wait till their very delapidation calls forth a voluntary contribution of cast-off garments; others, possessed with energy and love of neatness, ask for them whenever necessary. Nay, the "Profesh" make many a pretty penny on clothes thus obtained, which they sell to workingmen and Jews.

When out on the "Road," away from cities, the "Profesh" can always be told by their manner of sleeping. Realizing the worth of a good "front" (appearance), it behooves them to take good care of their apparel, so they have recourse to the newspaper blanket: Wherever they may select to sleep, they spread a newspaper or two on which to lie. Sleeping on the "road" in cold weather, the "Bindle Stiff" is the only comfortable tramp. The "Profesh," "Alki Stiffs," "Road-kids," etc. scorn carrying a "bindle" and needs must pay the consequence. But if a warm nook is to be had, trust them to find it. A favorite trick is their method of utilizing a refrigerator car. The walls of such a car are a foot thick, the doors fasten hermetically, and there is little or no ventilation. Once inside with the door closed, they make a bonfire of newspapers. As the heat, cannot escape, they sleep comfortably, and in the morning when they open the door, the inner is much warmer than the outer atmosphere.

The circulation of this great mass of human beings is an interesting phenomenon with which few of the upper world are conversant. Every spring the slums of the cities, the jails, poor houses, hospitals — the holes and dens in which the winter has been spent — give up their denizens who take to the "Road." This is the flux. All summer they wander, covering thousands upon thousands of miles, and with fall, crawl back to their holes and dens again — the ebb. Many blow whither they listeth: Many have definite plans. For instance, a tramp winters in New York City; starts out in the spring and travels to the north and west among the mining states; in the fall, goes south to Florida for the winter. Next summer finds him in Canada and the following winter in California. A third summer's wandering through the west and south, concludes with the warm weather of Mexico, where he laughs at winter terrors. This ebb and flow is also noticeable in the rushes to the great catastrophes, such as the Johnstown flood, the Charleston earthquake, the Chicago fire, and the St. Louis cyclone. There is also the periodical rush to the harvests and to the great fairs. At these places, for the "Profesh," is to be found rich loot; for the laboring tramp, work. Most pathetic is the return of the "Bindle Stiffs" from the harvest. They journey up into the Dakotas, and even into Manitoba, by the thousands, paying the brakemen half a dollar a division for the privilege of riding in empty box cars. They are essentially honest, hard-working laborers. All through the harvest they toil from dawn till dark, and at the season's close, are possessed of from one to three hundred dollars. They return in the same manner; but now they encounter the "Profesh," veritable beasts of the jungle. Perhaps half a dozen of them, having tipped the trainmen, are in a box car. Enter one or two "Profesh," who, at the pistol point, rob them of their year's wages. In the good old times, a single "Profesh" has often returned from three weeks of such work with two or three thousand dollars. This form of robbery is still perpetrated, but more rarely and with less remuneration. The resident population has increased, and fewer "Bindle Stiffs" are needed; while those who do earn money, usually send it back by mail or Wells Fargo.

Their *argot* is peculiar study. While in some instances it resembles that of "Chimmie Fadden," in most, it is widely different. Truly has Hugo said of *argot,* "Each accursed race has deposited its stratum, each suffering has dropped its stone, each heart has given its pebble." The sources of much are easily to be traced. *Kibosh* means utter discomfiture, from the Chinook; *galway* — priest — from the Gaelic; *bobbie* — policeman — transplanted from Cockney *argot; monica* — cognomen — a distorted version, both in form and meaning, of monogram; *star-route* — a "side jump" away from railroads — can be traced to the asterisks which denote Pony Express stations, and to steering and traveling by the heavenly constellations, when from the latter it is usually called a *star-light. Sou-markee* is a distorted combination from two root languages. It is a hyperbolical synonym for the smallest absolute coin and is used thus: — I haven't a *sou-markee.* The derivation is obvious. *Pounding the ear* means to sleep; *gondola,* flat car; *pogy,* poor house; *jerk,* a branch road or one little traveled; *glam,* steal; *gat,* gun, *shiv,* knife, *faune,* false; *crimpy,* cold; *dorse* or *kip,* to sleep; *queens,* women; *punk* or *dummy,* bread. One may understand the ordinary tramp, but it is often impossible to even comprehend the very "Profesh." Attempt to translate this: — *De stem? Nit! Yaeggin's on the sugar train. Hit a fly on the main-drag for a light piece; de bull snared me; got a t'ree hour blin'.* Here is a free version: — The street for begging? It is worthless. On the main street I begged a policeman in citizen's clothes for a small sum, but he (fly) (bull) (policeman) arrested me and the judge gave me three hours in which to leave town.

The tramp problem opens a vast field for study. In our high civilization it is a phenomenon, unique and paradoxical. Cause and cure have received countless explanations; but of one thing we must all be certain; and that, that work is not to be had for them. If they were annihilated, our industries would not suffer — nay, our army of unemployed would still be so large that wages would not rise. Capital being crystallized labor, it is axiomatic that labor produces more than it consumes. Hence, many must be idle; and, since through invention the efficiency of labor is constantly increasing, so must this army of idlers increase — of course, fluctuating as trade fluctuates. Is this true or is it not? Can the tramp be abolished or can he not? Is he an attendant evil on our civilization in certain stages of development or a permanent one? This is the problem: Is it to be solved?

"Jack London in Boston"

London submitted this essay to the Boston Evening Transcript *one week before it was published and received $20.00 for the article. "No. 2. Magazine Sales. From May 1900 to February 1903," Box 19, JCLC, USU, mistakenly states that he received 2¢ per word for the 2100-word essay.) In 1904 and again in 1909 London tried to place his reminiscence in England, but he was unsuccessful. "Magazine Sales #1," uncatalogued addendum to the JLP, HEH.*

How did I arrive in Boston? Let me see. It was in 1894, the year after the World's Fair, and somewhere along in the fall. Ah! how it comes back! I bid goodby to the City Hall park and the Bowery and left Harlem on a freight train which pulled out in two sections — the Old Colony railroad, I think; no, I don't remember, but anyway it ran to Boston. It was a Sunday afternoon, blazing with sunshine, so I had the pleasure of being thrown off the first and second sections by the "shacks." I beg pardon, "shack" is the vernacular for "brakeman." But in the third section was a "gondola" (flat car), loaded with huge iron pipes. Into one of these I curled up and read the New York Sunday papers, and, as the light waned, dozed off and regained the sleep lost the previous night in the company of a pessimistic printer out of a job.

Somewhere about midnight the train made a long stop in the railroad yards of some big city, and I crawled out long enough to borrow some tobacco from a sleepy wheel-tapper. What city it was I do not know. And for that matter, I do not know what part of

Source: "Jack London in Boston: Reminiscence by the author of the 'Son of Wolf.'" Boston *Evening Transcript,* May 26, 1900, p. 32.

the country I traversed during the trip — in all likelihood Connecticut and Rhode Island, but I have never taken the trouble to look
it up on the map. Suffice to say, having mulcted the aforesaid
wheel-tapper of half a sack of flake cut (excellent for cigarettes),
I caught my gondola and went to bed again.

The freight was leisurely pulling out of some small stop
when the next day broke, cold and gray, and found a "shack"
ill-manneredly hammering upon my iron pipe and inviting me
in no uncertain tone to "hit the grit." In other words, I was in
imminent danger of being forcibly ejected from a moving train.
Such things are not pleasant; so I bandied words with the man,
criticised his general make-up, and dissertated upon the vascular
action of the heart and the physiological cataclysms caused by
intemperate anger. I also commented upon his ancestry and
blackened his genealogical tree. As behooved a tramp of parts,
my master of intensive adjectives and vituperative English was such
as invariably to move men in my direction. This was what I desired,
and the man proceeded to do by crawling in after me. On the
outside he controlled both exits (a pipe having two ends), but once
inside he surrendered this tactical advantage. So I withdrew by
the opposite end, hastily, and "hit the grit" on my own feet, which
is a nicer way to alight, when all things are taken into consideratiou.
If that "shack" should cast his eyes upon this, let him rest assured
that I bore no malice — nay, not even when I made his soul bitter
with hypothetical epithets concerning the ways of his progenitors.

However, I found the town in which I had alighted to be
Attleboro, a place where the inhabitants solved the scheme of life
by manufacturing jewelry. As a traveller and a student of eco-
nomics and sociology, it was perhaps my duty to visit those estab-
lishments, but I preferred going round to the back doors of the
more imposing residences. After breakfasting with a pretty matron
and charming, to whom I had never been introduced and with
whom I failed to leave my card, I returned to the depot, where
I knew east-bound trains ran to Boston. It was raining, and I sought
shelter on the covered platform and rolled a cigarette. This action,
being essentially Californian, at once aroused attention, and forth-

with I was surrounded by a group of curious idlers, anxious to see the performance repeated. This was in 1894, so I suppose they have in the interim grown sufficiently degenerate to roll their own cigarettes. Nevertheless, I often wonder if any of them recollect the lad with the gray suit and cloth cap, smooth-faced and badly sunburned, who taught them how to do the trick.

I missed a train while out rustling dinner, then fell asleep in the waiting-room that evening and missed another, so that it was nearly midnight before I caught an eastbound freight and rode the decks (roofs) into the Hub. Now I must be treated leniently if it chanced that I saw but the surface of Boston. Remember, I was devoid of letters of credit or introduction, while my only entree was the police station. Entertaining peculiar tenets regarding cleanliness, it is not to be wondered that I avoided this place and sought a park bench instead. I wandered hit or miss till I came to the Common. And I knew it was the Common as soon as I put my eye upon it — why? I do not know. It must have been an inspiration.

Brrr! It's a raw old wind that blows in Boston, about 2 A.M., especially along in September, I shivered and shook, collar pulled up and cap down, vainly trying to sleep, till a policeman tapped me. Now, gentle reader, a word of warning should you ever go on the "road": Always placate the policeman. He is at once the dispenser and obfuscator of life, liberty and the pursuit of happiness. He shapes the destinies of lesser creatures, and free air or dungeon lurk in his gruff "Move on," or "Come on." Placate him by all means, when your trails cross, and one way to do this is to arouse his interest. This I endeavored to do in the present instance by simulating drowsiness and by mumbling unintelligibly:

"What?" he peremptorily demanded, and I answered, "Oh, never mind. I wasn't awake yet, and I was dreaming about Ueno Park."

"Where's that?" he asked, and when I replied, "Japan," I had him. And for two solid hours I led him up hill and down dale, in Yokohama and Tokio, on Fujiyama, through tea house and temple, bazaar and marketplace, till he forgot the municipality he served and the malefactors who feared him. At the end of that time he discovered that my teeth were chattering, said he was sorry he hadn't any whiskey about him, gave me a silver quarter instead, and departed — he and his club.

Like Mowgli of undying fame, I had wandered through a thousand villages, and, like him, never had I been lost. But that was all in the golden days before I ventured on the cow paths of Boston. With the policeman's silver quarter burning my hand, and in my eyes a vision of steaming coffee and juicy steak, I hastened forth in search of an all-night restaurant. This latter I found without difficulty, but not so the Common. For the rest of the night I wandered in quest of it, looking always for it to appear at the next crooked turning; but the powers had decreed that two days should elapse before I again clapped eyes on it.

Some time after daylight I found myself on the bridge which goes to Charlestown. As the breakfast hour approaches, men under similar circumstances to mine always point their toes in the direction of the residence districts. The street is a poor place for coppers in the early morning, while the belly-need is a strenuous thing for a healthy man to carry around with him. On the bridge I overtook one of the fraternity. If by nothing else, I classified him by the look of his eye.

"You're no gay cat," he remarked, after a comprehensive glance. "One of the profesh, of course."

I signified in the appropriate terms that such was my rating, and we unified our pace.

"New to the town, eh?" he asked. "I thought so. Came in last night? How'd you find floppings? Pretty crimpy, eh? Well, I know the old jerk like a book, and I'll put you wise. Going to throw your feet for Java? I'll put you on."

And in this wise he manifested the good comradeship of the "Road." Translated into common parlance, he had given me to understand that he divined I was a professional hobo, just arrived; that in my ignorance of the place I had got poor quarters and slept coldly; also that I was out in search of breakfast and that he would direct me to houses known as good. Yet this tramp, as I afterwards learned, was an erstwhile gentleman and college man, with more knowledge and culture under his rags than falls to the average man who sits in the high places.

As it was rather early, we sunned ourselves on the benches beside the Bunker Hill Monument, and, discovering an affinity of tastes and studies, discussed till breakfast time the possibilities of a reconciliation of Kant and Spencer. After having satisfied the material man by "slamming gates" and "back-door collections," we returned to the monument. Here we took the sunshine and talked Karl Marx and the German economists, until, in a sort of bashful way, he announced the possession of antiquarian propensities. Thereat I was haled across the bridge to the North End, where he resurrected all manner of architectural antiquities and fairly bubbled with the histories of the old buildings. How he ever acquired it all — the local knowledge and tradition — puzzled me; for he was Southern born and had been in Boston but little over six weeks.

Two days I spent with this most entertaining person, putting much of our time into the North End, but wherever we happened to go, going with antiquities in prospect. Most of the relics are long since forgotten, but I shall never forget how lovingly and eloquently he dwelt upon the histories of such places as the Granary Burial Ground, the Old State House, the Old South Church and the house of Paul Revere. Needless to speak of my delight in all this, for I was fresh from the "new and naked lands" of the great West, where the elder inhabitants antedated history, and there was nothing old save the soil.

But I lost him one day, as men will lose comrades on the "Road," and next picked up with a Dissolute Plumber's Apprentice of Celtic descent and cursed with the Curse of Reuben. He had read Arthur McEven's "San Francisco News Letter," and my heart warmed to him. He was possessed of the more modern spirit, exulted in modernity in fact, and bent his efforts toward showing me the latest achievements and newest improvements. I remember he particularly dilated upon Boston's park system, and took me to the public gymnasiums. And he it was who led my erring feet back to the Common. But I had one fault to find with him, and only one.

He persisted in the belief that because I hailed from the West I could not take care of myself in a metropolis like Boston. His solicitude for me on a street crossing was side-bursting. Especially did he fear that I would be run down by that strange and terrible contrivance, the electric car.

But the best of friends must part. I had my eyes fixed upon Montreal and Ottawa, and winter was coming on. So the Dissolute Plumber's Apprentice went down with me to the railroad yards, cursing the while his lack of soul for great hazards and his instability of purpose which prevented him accompanying me. He gave me his address, and some day I would write to him, did I not feel certain that the exigencies of his status have long since forced him to change his abode a score of times.

As he gripped my hand for the last time, he said, feelingly, "Good-by, Jack, and say, old man, never will I forget the superb nonchalance with which you rolled a cigarette while an electric car nearly ripped you up the back."

That night it turned very cold, so I forsook my tenets and slept in the police station in Lawrence.

"The Worker and the Tramp"

No information is available concerning the writing of this poem. But Robert H. Woodward cites its reprinting in Discover the Friendly City — Oakland *in July 1970 as an indication of the work's contemporary relevance. He contends that the poem was utilized to show the inequity between white and black unemployment in Oakland. The emphasis in the poem, says Woodward, fits exactly with recent conditions. See his brief essay "Jack London as Poet-Reformer: A New Reprint,"* London Collector *Broadside Number One, 1971 (Cedar Springs, Michigan).*

Heaven bless you, my friend —
   You, the man who won't sweat;
Here's a quarter to spend.

If you did but mend,
   My job you would get; —
Heaven bless you, my friend. —

On you I depend
   For my work don't forget; —
Here's a quarter to spend.

Your course I commend,
   Nor regard with regret; —
Heaven bless you, my friend.

Source: *The Comrade,* I (October 1901), 14.

My hand I extend,
　　For I love you, you bet; —
Here's a quarter to spend.

Ah! you comprehend
　　That I owe you a debt;
Heaven bless you, my friend,
Here's a quarter to spend.

"Rods and Gunnels"

London tried to sell this sketch to four magazines, including Harper's Weekly *and* Saturday Evening Post, *before* The Bookman *accepted the 2500-word essay for $20.00 in April of 1902. He was unable to place the piece in England, although he attempted to do so in 1904 and 1909. "No. 2. Magazine Sales. From May 1900 to Feb. 1903," Box 19, JCLC, USU; No. 3 Magazine Sales, Feb. 1903 — July, Box 102, JLP, HEH.*

He who knows but one class of tramps can no more understand that class of tramps than he who knows but one language can understand that language. This is indisputable. And out of this non-misunderstanding, or partial understanding, much erroneous information is given forth to those who do not know tramps at all. And not only is this unjust to those who do not know, but it is unjust to the tramp. It is the intention of this brief article to correct some of this misinformation; and it is as an old-time tramp, a "comet," one who has served his "road-kid" and "gay-cat" apprenticeship, that I shall speak thus authoritatively.

When I say that the average tramp does not understand Trampland, it will be readily understood that the average sociologist, tentatively dabbling, does not and cannot understand Trampland. A single instance of this should suffice. Now it is notorious that Eastern tramps do not know how to "railroad." The tramp whose habitat has been confined to the East and South can no more "hold down" a train in spite of a "horstile" crew than can he step into Rockefeller's office and "hold down" Standard Oil. Conditions do not demand it. He is not trained to it. The crews are rarely

Source: *The Bookman,* XV (August 1902), 541-544.

"horstile." Speaking out of my own experience, I have been but twice put off trains between the Mississippi and the Atlantic Ocean; while west of the Mississippi I have been put off, and thrown off, and beaten off more times than I can recollect.

But the instance I have in mind. In professional Trampland the United States over, "riding the rods" has a specific meaning. It characterises, not various kinds of acts, but one particular act. Yet the average Eastern tramp and the average Eastern tramp-investigator do not know what this particular act is. The ordinary tramp hears the professional tramp, the comet, or the tramp-royal, speak of "riding the rods," and, utterly ignorant of what the rods are (because he has never had to ride them), he confuses them with the gunnels and concludes that he, too, has "ridden the rods." And not only this, for he describes the operation to the tramp-investigator, poses on the gunnels before a camera, and the erroneous picture is reproduced in our magazines, labeled "Riding the Rods."

Now, what are the gunnels? As correctly described but incorrectly named, they are "the truss rods which, after the fashion of bridge trusses, support the middle stretch of the car between trucks." They are heavy iron rods which run lengthwise with the car, and which differ in number and shape according to the make of the car. While they occur on passenger coaches, no one ever dreams of riding them except on freight cars. And by those who know and who set the pace in Trampland, they are named "gunnels." And be it remarked parenthetically that criteria are required in Trampland as well as any other land. Somebody must set the pace, give the law, sanction usage.

Anybody with arms and legs can ride the gunnels. It requires no special trick or nerve, and this in the face of the dictum of the ordinary tramp (the "gay-cat" and stew-bum), who swells pridefully and narrates valorously in the presence of the stray and passing sociologist.

But to "ride the rods" requires nerve, and skill, and daring. And, by the way, there is but one rod, and it occurs on passenger coaches. Idiomatically, it becomes "rods," just as idiomatically we speak of "riding trains." As a matter of fact, I have never yet met a man who made a practice of riding more than one train at a time. But to return. One never rides the gunnels on "passengers"; one never rides the rods on "freights." Also, between the rod on a "four-wheeler" and the rod on a "six-wheeler" there is the difference of life and death.

A four-wheel truck is oblong in shape, and is divided into halves by a cross-partition. What is true of one-half is true of the other half. Between this cross-partition and the axle is a small lateral rod, three to four feet in length, running parallel with both the partition and the axle. This is the *rod*. There is more often than not another rod, running longitudinally, the air-brake rod. These rods cross each other; but woe to the tyro who takes his seat on the brake-rod! It is not *the* rod, and the chance is large that the tyro's remains will worry and puzzle the county coroner.

Let me explain how such a rod is ridden. One may take his seat on it when the train is stationary. This is comparatively easy. But the "comet" and the "profesh," the men who ride despite "horstile" crews, are wont to take their seats while the train is under way. This is how it is done, and since I have done it often, for clearness let me describe it in the first person:

The train is pulling out and going as fast as a man can run, or even faster. Time, night or day; to one who is familiar it does not matter. I stand alongside the track. The train is approaching. With a quick eye I select the coach and truck — the for'ard truck, so that, sheltered by the cross-partition, I shall avoid "punching the wind." I begin to run gently in the direction the train is going. As "my" truck comes closer I hit up my pace, and just before it reaches me I make one swift spurt, so that when it is abreast of me the respective velocities of the train and myself are nearly equalised. At this moment (and it must be the moment of moments and neither the moment before nor the moment after), at this moment I suddenly stoop, reach under the car and seize hold of the first gunnel; and at this same instant I lift my feet from the ground, swing my body under the car and bring my feet to rest on the brake-beam. The posture is undignified and perilous. My feet are merely resting, my whole weight is supported by my arms, the car above me is rolling and jolting, and my back is toward the rails singing beneath.

But, hand over hand, I haul myself in till I am standing in a doubled position on the brake-beam. It will be noted that I am still *outside* the truck. Between the top of the truck and the bottom of the car is a narrow space, barely sufficient to admit a man's body. Through this I squeeze, in such manner that my feet still remain *outside* the truck on the brake beam, my stomach is pressed against the *top* of the truck, and my head and shoulders unsupported, are *inside* the truck, I say "unsupported," and I mean it, for beneath my chest is the rapidly revolving axle. This I dare not touch, but must thrust my head and trunk, snake fashion, over and past it and down till I can lay my hands on either the brake-rod or the cross-rod. This done, my head and shoulders are now lower than my hips (which are on top the truck), and I must draw my hips, legs and feet over and down across that moving axle without touching. Squirming and twisting, this is accomplished, and I sit down on the cross-rod, back resting against the side of the truck, one shoulder against the cross-partition, the other shoulder within a couple of inches of the whirling wheel. My legs are disposed along the rod to where my feet rest on it at the opposite end within an inch or so of the other wheel. More than once I have had a wheel rasp against my shoe or whizz greasily on my shoulder. Six or eight inches beneath me are the ties, bounding along at thirty, forty, or fifty miles an hour, and all in the world between is a slender swaying rod as thick as a man's first finger. Dirt and gravel are flying, the car is bounding overhead, the earth flashing away beneath, there is clank and clash, and rumble and roar, and . . . this is "riding the rods."

As I write I have before me my "ticket." I have ridden countless miles on it. It is a piece of three-quarter-inch pine, well seasoned, four inches wide by five long. Across it a rude groove has been gashed with a jack-knife. Into this groove the rod fits, and on this piece of wood the man sits. It is a small affair. When not in use I carried it in my hip pocket. Yet I have seen the passing sociologist and tramp-investigator, in the course of mis-describing rod-riding, speak of "tickets" which were four-foot planks!

I remember being "ditched" on a little "jerk" road in the French country near Montreal. With me were two other "stiffs," Vancouver Ned and Chi Slim. Vancouver Ned was a tramp-royal. He was just back from across the pond and was returning to Vancouver. Chi Slim, as his "monica" denotes, hailed from Chicago. He thought of himself as a "blowed in-the-glass stiff," and so far as his experience went he was so blown, but his experience was quite limited. His seven years of tramping had been narrowly confined. He was not a product of rigid selection. A certain repressed eagerness alternated with fits of timidity, and one could see at a glance that this was his first big adventure. He had broken out of his habitat and was at last on the great "road." And as befitted one honoured by the companionship of a "comet" and a tramp-royal, he deemed it necessary to put on a wise "front." He was a bold, bad man, and the chests he threw amused Vancouver Ned and me. Since he was bound West, we knew he stood in need of education, and Vancouver Ned kindly proceeded to "put him wise" concerning the "railroading" he would have to do ere he achieved West. Vancouver Ned mentioned riding the rods as necessary for getting over the ground. Oh, he knew all about riding the rods, did Chi Slim; he was no "gay cat." I saw that he needed fetching down a peg or so, told him that I knew he did not know, and challenged him to go down to the railroad yards and show us the rods. He led the way confidently, and, as we had suspected, pointed in triumph to the gunnels!

Another current and widespread misconception is that the train crews (the "shacks"), if they wished, could prevent all tramps from riding. It is undeniable that if they tried they could prevent many tramps from riding, but it is deniable that they could prevent all. There are probably some several thousand tramps in the United States who can successfully defy any such attempt, while the very attempt would develop many thousand more — the men who "hold down" trains in spite of the crews "horstile" or otherwise. I have forced an Overland Mail to stop five times, and then indulged the anxious-eyed passengers with a rough-and-tumble with the "shacks" before I was finally "ditched." But this was in broad daylight and I was handicapped. Had it been night time, barring accidents, they could not have kept me off. But they were carrying the mails, and a policy of stopping five times for every tramp along the track is on the face of it absurd. As Josiah Flynt has pointed out to completely rid a railroad of tramps a police service is necessary. The trainmen have other functions to perform. And as to the brakemen being passively consenting parties to the free freightage of hobos, well, and what of it? It's easier to than not to; and further, more than one over-zealous "shack" has been strewn in fragments along the right of way by tramps who elected to become "horstile."

The point of this article is: *that when the lesser local tramps are themselves ignorant of much of the real "road," the stray and passing sociologist, dealing only with the lesser local tramps, must stand in corresponding ignorance.* Such investigators do not deal with the genuine "profesh." The tramps they probe and dissect are mere creatures, without perspective, incapable of "sizing up" or understanding the Underworld in which they live. These are the *canaille* and *bourgeoisie,* these "gay cats," "bindle stiffs," "stake men," "shovel bums," "mushers," "fakirs" and "stew bums." As well might the Man from Mars get a lucid and philosophic exposition of twentieth-century sublunary society from a denizen of Mulberry Street as the stray and passing sociologist get a clear and searching exposition of the "road" from these men.

The "profesh" do not lend themselves to putting inquisitive "mugs" wise. They do not lend themselves to putting any one wise save their own "prushuns." Nor can the superficial investigator come to know the "profesh" by merely "hitting the road." So far as they are concerned, he will be despised, as a "gay cat," or in more familiar parlance, as a short horn, a tenderfoot, a new chum. He cannot know the "profesh" until he has hobnobbed with them, and he cannot hobnob with them until he has qualified. And he may be so made that he can never qualify. Thousands of men on the "road" are unfit to be "profesh"; it is impossible for them to be "profesh." The "profesh" are the aristocracy of their Underworld. They are the lords and masters, the aggressive men, the primordial noble men, the *blond beasts* of Neitzsche, lustfully roving and conquering through sheer superiority and strength. Unwritten is the law they impose. They are the Law, the Law incarnate. And the Underworld looks up to them and obeys. They are not easy of access. They are conscious of their own nobility and treat only with equals. Unless the investigator qualify, as Josiah Flynt qualified ("The Cigarette"), he will never know them. And unless he be able to qualify and know them, he will be no fit exponent of the Underworld to the Upperworld.

"How I became a Socialist"

London presented this essay as a gift to The Comrade *in February of 1903. There is no evidence he tried to sell it in the United States, but it was sold in England to* Westminster Gazette *for 5/5/0. "No. 2. Magazine Sales. From May 1900 to Feb. 1903," Box 19, JCLC, USU; Magazine Sales #3, JLP, HEH.*

It is quite fair to say that I became a Socialist in a fashion somewhat similar to the way in which the Teutonic pagans became Christians — it was hammered into me. Not only was I not looking for Socialism at the time of my conversion, but I was fighting it. I was very young and callow, did not know much of anything, and though I had never even heard of a school called "Individualism," I sang the pæan of the strong with all my heart.

This was because I was strong myself. By strong I mean that I had good health and hard muscles, both of which possessions are easily accounted for. I had lived my childhood on California ranches, my boyhood hustling newspapers on the streets of a healthy Western city, and my youth on the ozone-laden waters of San Francisco Bay and the Pacific Ocean. I loved life in the open, and I toiled in the open, at the hardest kinds of work. Learning no trade, but drifting along from job to job, I looked on the world and called it good, every bit of it. Let me repeat, this optimism was because I was healthy and strong, bothered with neither aches nor weaknesses, never turned down by the boss because I did not look fit, able always to get a job at shoveling coal, sailorizing, or manual labor of some sort.

And because of all this, exulting in my young life, able to hold

---

Source: *The Comrade,* II (March 1903), 122-123.

my own at work or fight, I was a rampant individualist. It was very natural. I was a winner. Wherefore I called the game, as I saw it played, or thought I saw it played, a very popular game for Men. To be a MAN was to write man in large capitals on my heart. To adventure like a man, and fight like a man, and do a man's work (even for a boy's pay) — these were things that reached right in and gripped hold of me as no other thing could. And I looked ahead into long vistas of a hazy and interminable future, into which, playing what I conceived to be MAN'S game, I should continue to travel with unfailing health, without accidents, and with muscles ever vigorous. As I say, this future was interminable. I could only see myself raging through life without end like one of Nietzsche's *blond beasts,* lustfully roving and conquering by sheer superiority and strength.

As for the unfortunates, the sick, and ailing, and old, and maimed, I must confess I hardly thought of them at all, save that I vaguely felt that they, barring accidents, could be as good as I if they wanted to real hard, and could work just as well. Accidents? Well, they represented FATE, also spelled out in capitals, and there was no getting around FATE. Napoleon had had an accident at Waterloo, but that did not dampen my desire to be another and later Napoleon. Further, the optimism bred of a stomach which could digest scrap iron and a body which flourished on hardships did not permit me to consider accidents as even remotely related to my glorious personality.

I hope I have made it clear that I was proud to be one of Nature's strong-armed noblemen. The dignity of labor was to me the most impressive thing in the world. Without having read Carlyle, or Kipling, I formulated a gospel of work which put theirs in the shade. Work was everything. It was sanctification and salvation. The pride I took in a hard day's work well done would be inconceivable to you. It is almost inconceivable to me as I look back upon it. I was as faithful a wage slave as ever capitalist exploited. To shirk or malinger on the man who paid me my wages was a sin, first, against myself, and second, against him. I considered it a crime second only to treason and just about as bad.

In short, my joyous individualism was dominated by the orthodox bourgeois ethics. I read the bourgeois papers, listened to the bourgeois preachers, and shouted at the sonorous platitudes of the bourgeois politicians. And I doubt not, if other events had not changed my career, that I should have evolved into a professional strike-breaker (one of President Eliot's American heroes), and had my head and my earning power inrrevocably smashed by a club in the hands of some militant trades-unionist.

Just about this time, returning from a seven months' voyage before the mast, and just turned eighteen, I took it into my head to go tramping. On rods and blind baggages I fought my way from the open West, where men bucked big and the job hunted the man, to the congested labor centers of the East, where men were small potatoes and hunted the job for all they were worth. And on this new *blond-beast* adventure I found myself looking upon life from a new and totally different angle. I had dropped down from the proletariat into what sociologists love to call the "submerged tenth," and I was startled to discover the way in which that submerged tenth was recruited.

I found there all sorts of men, many of whom had once been as good as myself and just as *blond-beastly;* sailormen, soldier-men, labor-men, all wrenched and distorted and twisted out of shape by toil and hardship and accident, and cast adrift by their masters like so many old horses. I battered on the drag and slammed back gates with them, or shivered with them in box cars and city parks, listening the while to life histories which began under auspices as fair as mine, with digestions and bodies equal to and better than mine, and which ended there before my eyes in the shambles at the bottom of the Social Pit.

And as I listened my brain began to work. The woman of the streets and the man of the gutter drew very close to me. I saw the picture of the Social Pit as vividly as though it were a concrete thing, and at the bottom of the Pit I saw them, myself above them, not far, and hanging on to the slippery wall by main strength and sweat. And I confess a terror seized me. What when my strength failed? when I would be unable to work shoulder to shoulder with the strong men who were as yet babes unborn? And there and then I swore a great oath. It ran something like this: *All my days I have worked hard with my body, and according to the number of days I have worked, by just that much am I nearer the bottom of the Pit. I shall climb out of the Pit, but not by the muscles of my body shall I climb out. I shall do no more hard work, and may God strike me dead if I do another day's hard work with my body more than I absolutely have to.* And I have been busy ever since running away from hard bodily labor.

Incidentally, while tramping some ten thousand miles through the United States and Canada, I strayed into Niagara Falls, was nabbed by a fee-hunting constable, denied the right to plead guilty or not guilty, sentenced out of hand to thirty days' imprisonment for having no fixed abode and no visible means of support, hand-cuffed and chained to a bunch of men similarly circumstanced, carted down country to Buffalo, registered at the Erie County Penitentiary, had my head clipped and my budding mustache shaved, was dressed in convict stripes, compulsorily vaccinated by a medical student who practiced on such as we, made to march the lock-step, and put to work under the eyes of guards armed with Winchester rifles — all for adventuring in *blond-beastly* fashion. Concerning further details deponent sayeth not, though he may hint that some of his plethoric national patriotism simmered down and leaked out of the bottom of his soul somewhere— at least, since that experience he finds that he cares more for men and women and little children than for imaginary geographical lines.

To return to my conversion. I think it is apparent that my rampant individualism was pretty effectively hammered out of me, and something else as effectively hammered in. But, just as I had been an individualist without knowing it, I was now a Socialist without knowing it, withal, an unscientific one. I had been reborn, but not renamed, and I was running around to find out what manner of thing I was. I ran back to California and opened the books. I do not remember which ones I opened first. It is an unimportant detail anyway. I was already It, whatever It was, and by aid of the books I discovered that It was a Socialist. Since that day I have opened many books, but no economic argument, no lucid demonstration of the logic and inevitableness of Socialism affects me as profoundly and convincingly as I was affected on the day when I first saw the walls of the Social Pit rise around me and felt myself slipping down, down into the shambles at the bottom.

"Local Color"

London *first sent this story to* McClure's, *but one of the editors of the magazine returned the story — along with the essay "The Tramp," which had also been submitted to* McClure's *— stating "we cannot use these" (John S. Phillips to London, December 20, 1901, Box 46, JLP, HEH). London followed his usual practice of not revising the story but keeping it in the mail to other magazines. Four other editors rejected the story before he sent it to* Atlantic Monthly *in March of 1902. When George Brett, London's publisher at Macmillan, asked to see the story, London wrote: "The tramp story, which you mention, is only the first one of a series which I have discontinued. It is with the* Atlantic *just now, or I would let you see it, though, really, I have become chary of letting anyone see it" (Letters, p. 134). Bliss Perry, the editor of* Atlantic, *returned the story and told London: "The tramp story does not particularly tempt us, although we recognize the extreme skill which you have shown in putting it together (Perry to London, April 24, 1902, Box 46, JLP, HEH.*

Though London professed to have misgivings about the story, he sent the tale to five other publishers in the next ten months before Ainslee's *accepted it in March of 1903. Perhaps he was able to sell the story to* Ainslee's *because he owed the magazine $150.00 ("No. 2. Magazine Sales. From May 1900 to Feb. 1903," Box 19, JCLC, USU). When an interviewer asked London about the origins of the tale, he replied that " 'the story in itself was a true one, depicting an episode in the life of a tramp journalist, if I may use the term." 'Dan Riley, "A Chat with Jack London,"* Pastime Magazine *[Chicago], April 1906.*

Source: *Ainslee's* XII (October 1903), 74-82.

"I do not see why you should not turn this immense amount of unusual information to account," I told him. "Unlike most men equipped with similar knowledge, *you* have expression. Your style is — "

"Is sufficiently — er — journalese," he interrupted suavely.

"Precisely! You could turn a pretty penny."

But he interlocked his fingers meditatively, shrugged his shoulders, and dismissed the subject.

"I have tried it. It does not pay.

"It was paid for and published," he added, after a pause. "And I was also honored with sixty days in the *Hobo.*"

"The *Hobo?*" I ventured.

"The *Hobo* . . ." He fixed his eyes on my Spencer and ran along the titles while he cast his definition. "The *Hobo,* my dear fellow, is the name for that particular place of detention in city and county jails, wherein are assembled tramps, drunks, beggars, and the riffraff of petty offenders. The word itself is a pretty one, and it has a history. *Hautbois* — there's the French of it. *Haut,* meaning high, and *bois,* wood. In English it becomes hautboy, a wooden musical instrument of two foot tone, I believe, played with a double reed; an oboe, in fact. You remember in 'Henry IV':

> " 'The case of a treble hautboy was a mansion for him,
>   a court.'

"From this to ho-boy is but a step, and for that matter the English used the terms interchangeably. But — and mark you, the leap paralyzes one — crossing the Western Ocean, in York City hautboy, or ho boy, becomes the name by which the night scavenger is known. In a way one understands its being born of the contempt for wandering players and musical fellows. But see the beauty of it! The burn and the brand! The night scavenger, the pariah, the miserable, the despised, the man without caste — and in its next incarnation, consistently and logically, it attaches itself to the American outcast, namely, the tramp. Then, as others have mutilated its sense, the tramp mutilates its form, and ho-boy becomes exultantly hobo. Wherefore, the large stone and brick cells, lined with double and triple-tiered bunks, in which the law is wont to incarcerate him, he calls the *Hobo*. Interesting, isn't it?"

And I sat back and marveled secretly at this encyclopædic-minded man, this Leith Clay-Randolph, this common tramp who made himself at home in my den, charmed such friends as gathered at my small table, outshone me with his brilliance and his manners, spent my spending money, smoked my best cigars, and selected from my ties and studs with a cultivated and discriminating eye.

He absently walked over to the shelves and looked into Loria's "Economic Foundations of Society."

"I like to talk with you," he remarked. "You are not indifferently schooled. You've read the books, and your economic interpretation of history, as you choose to call it" (this with a sneer) "eminently fits you for an intellectual outlook on life. But your sociologic judgments are vitiated by your lack of practical knowledge. Now I, who know the books, pardon me, somewhat better than you, know life, too. I have lived it, naked, taken it up in both my hands and looked at it, and tasted it, the flesh and the blood of it, and being purely an intellectual, I have been biased by neither passion nor prejudice. **All of which is** necessary for clear concepts, and all of which you lack. Ah! a really clever passage. Listen!"

And he read aloud to me in his remarkable manner, paralleling the text with a running criticism and commentary, lucidly wording involved and lumbering periods, casting side and cross lights upon the subject, introducing points the author had blundered past and objections he had ignored, catching up lost ends, flinging a contrast into a paradox and reducing it to a coherent and succinctly stated truth — in short, flashing his luminous genius in a blaze of fire over pages erstwhile dull and heavy and lifeless.

It is long since that Leith Clay-Randolph (note the hyphenated surname) knocked at the back door of Idlewild and melted the heart of Gunda. Now Gunda was cold as her Norway hills, and in her least frigid moods was even capable of permitting especially nice-looking tramps to sit on the back stoop and devour lone crusts and forlorn and forsaken chops. But that a tatterdemalion out of the night should invade the sanctity of her kitchen-kingdom and delay dinner while she set a place for him in the warmest corner, was a matter of such moment that the Sunflower went to see. Ah, the Sunflower, of the soft heart and swift sympathy! Leith Clay-Randolph threw his glamour over her for fifteen long minutes, while I brooded with my cigar, and then she fluttered back with vague words and the suggestion of a cast-off suit I would never miss.

"Surely I shall never miss it," I said, and I had in mind the dark gray suit with the pockets draggled from the freightage of many books, books which had spoiled more than one day's fishing sport.

"I should advise you, however," I added, "to mend the pockets first."

But the Sunflower's face clouded.

"N-o," she said, "the black one."

"The black one!" This explosively, incredulously. "I wear it quite often. I — I intended wearing it to-night."

"You have two better ones, and you know I never liked it, dear," the Sunflower hurried on. "Besides, it's shiny — "

"Shiny!"

"It — it soon will be, which is just the same, and the man is really estimable. He is nice and refined, and I am sure he — "

"Has seen better days."

"Yes, and the weather is raw and beastly, and his clothes are threadbare. And you have many suits — "

"Five," I corrected, "counting in the dark gray fishing outfit with the draggled pockets."

"And he has none, no home, nothing — "

"Not even a sunflower" — putting my arm around her — "wherefore he is deserving of all things. Give him the black suit, dear — nay the best one, the very best one. Under high heaven for such lack there must be compensation!"

"You *are* a dear!" And the Sunflower fluttered to the door and looked back alluringly. "You are a *perfect* dear."

And this after seven years, I marveled, till she was back again, timid and apologetic.

"I— I gave him one of your white shirts. He wore a horrid cheap cotton thing, and I knew it would look ridiculous. And then his shoes were so slip-shod. I let him have a pair of yours, the old ones with the narrow caps — "

"*Old* ones!"

"Well, they pinched horribly, and you know they did."

It was ever thus the Sunflower vindicated things.

And so Leith Clay-Randolph came to Idlewild to stay, how long I did not dream. Nor how often, for like an erratic comet he came and went. Fresh he would arrive, and cleanly clad, from grand folk who were his friends as I was his friend, and again, weary and worn, he would creep up the briar-rose path from the Montanas or Mexico. And without a word, when his *wanderlust* gripped him, he was off and away into that great mysterious underworld he called "The Road."

"I could not bring myself to leave until I had thanked you, you of the open hand and heart," he said on the night he donned my good black suit.

And I confess I was startled when I glanced over the top of my paper and saw a lofty-browed and eminently respectable looking gentleman, boldly and carelessly at ease. The Sunflower was right. He must have known better days for the black suit and white shirt to have effected such a transformation. Involuntarily, I arose to my feet, prompted instinctively to meet him on equal ground. And then it was the Clay-Randolph glamour descended upon me. He slept at Idlewild that night, and the next night, and for many nights. And he was a man to love. The son of Anak, otherwise Rufus the Blue-Eyed, and also plebeianly known as Tots, rioted with him from briar-rose path to farthest orchard, scalped him in the haymow with barbaric yells, and once, with Pharisaic zeal, was near to crucifying him under the attic roof beams. The Sunflower would have loved him for the Son of Anak's sake, had she not loved him for his own. As for myself, let the Sunflower tell, in the times he elected to be gone, of how often I wondered when Leith would come back again, Leith the Lovable.

Yet he was a man of whom we knew nothing. Beyond the

fact that he was Kentucky-born, his past was a blank. He never spoke of it. And he was a man who prided himself upon his utter divorce of reason from emotion. To him the word spelled itself out in problems. I charged him once with being guilty of emotion when roaring around the den with the Son of Anak pic-a-back. Not so, he held. Could he not cuddle a sense-delight for the problem's sake?

He was elusive. A man who intermingled nameless argot with polysyllabic and technical terms, he would seem sometimes the veriest criminal, in speech, face, expression, everything; at other times the cultured and polished gentleman, and again, the philosopher and scientist. But there was something glimmering there which I never caught — flashes of sincerity, of real feeling, I imagined, which were sped ere I could grasp; echoes of the man he once was, possibly, or hints of the man behind the mask. But the mask he never lifted, and the real man we never knew.

"But the sixty days with which you were rewarded for your journalism?" I asked. "Never mind Loria. Tell me."

"Well, if I must." He flung one knee over the other and laughed shortly.

"In a town which shall be nameless," he began: "in fact, a city of fifty thousand, a fair and beautiful city wherein men slave for dollars and women for dress, an idea came to me. My *front* was prepossessing, as fronts go, and my pockets empty. I had in recollection a thought I once entertained of writing a reconciliation of Kant and Spencer. Not that they are reconcilable, of course, but the room offered for scientific satire — "

I waved my hand impatiently, and he broke off.

"I was just tracing my mental states for you in order to show the genesis of the action," he explained. "However, the idea came. What was the matter with a tramp sketch for the daily press? The Irreconcilability of the Constable and the Tramp, for instance? So I hit the *drag* (the drag, my dear fellow, is merely the street), or the high places if you will, for a newspaper office. The elevator whisked me into the sky, and Cerberus, in the guise of an anemic office boy, guarded the door. Consumption, one could see it at a glance: nerve, Irish, colossal; tenacity, undoubted; dead inside the year.

" 'Pale youth,' quoth I, 'I pray thee the way to the *sanctum sanctorum,* to the Most High Cock-a-lorum.'

"He deigned to look at me, scornfully, with infinite weariness.

" 'G'wan an' see the janitor. I don't know nothin' about the gas.'

" 'Nay, my lily-white, the editor.'

" 'Wich editor?' he snapped, like a young bull-terrier. 'Dramatic? Sportin'? Society? Sunday? Weekly? Daily? Telegraph? Local? News? Editorial? Wich?'

"Which, I did not know.

" '*The* Editor,' I proclaimed stoutly. 'The *only* Editor.'

" 'Aw, Spargo!' he sniffled.

" 'Of course, Spargo,' I answered. 'Who else?'

" 'Gimme yer card,' says he.

" 'My what?'

" 'Yer card — Say! Wot's yer business, anyway?'

"And the anæmic Cerberus sized me up with so insolent an eye that I reached over and took him out of his chair. I knocked on his meager chest with my fore knuckle and fetched forth a weak, gaspy cough, but he looked at me unflinchingly, much like a defiant sparrow held in the hand.

" 'I am the census-taker Time.' I boomed, in sepulchral tones. 'Beware lest I knock too loud.'

" 'Oh, I don't know,' he sneered.

"Whereupon I rapped him smartly, and he chocked and turned purplish.

" 'Well, whatcher want?' he wheezed with returning breath.

" 'I want Spargo, the only Spargo.'

" 'Then leave go, an' I'll glide an' see.'

" 'No you don't, my lily-white.' And I took a tighter grip on his collar. 'No bouncers in mine, understand! I'll go along.' "

Leith dreamily surveyed the long ash of his cigar and turned to me.

"Do you know, Anak, you can't appreciate the joy of being

the buffoon, playing the clown. You couldn't do it if you wished. Your pitiful little conventions and smug assumptions of decency would prevent. But to simply turn loose your soul to every whimsicality, to play the fool unafraid of any possible result, why that requires a man other than a householder and law-respecting citizen.

"However, as I was saying, I saw the only Spargo. He was a big, beefy, red-faced personage, full-jowled and double-chinned, sweating at his desk in his shirt sleeves. It was August, you know. He was talking into a telephone when I entered, or swearing rather, I should say, and the while studying me with his eyes. When he hung up he turned to me expectantly.

" 'You are a very busy man.' I said.

"He jerked a nod with his head, and waited.

" 'And after all, is it worth it?' I went on. 'What does life mean that it should make you sweat? What justification do you find in sweat? Now look at me. I toil not, neither do I spin — '

" 'Who are you? What are you?' he bellowed with a suddenness that was — well, rude, tearing the words out as a dog does a bone.

" 'A very pertinent question, sir.' I acknowledged. 'First, I am a man: next, a downtrodden American citizen. I am cursed with neither profession, trade, nor expectations. Like Esau, I am pottageless. My residence is everywhere; the sky is my coverlet. I am of the dispossessed, a *sansculotte,* a proletarian, or, in simpler phraseology addressed to your understanding, a tramp.'

" 'What the hell — ?'

" 'Nay, fair sir, a tramp a man of devious ways and strange lodgments and multifarious — '

" 'Quit it!' he shouted. 'What do you want?'

" 'I want money.'

"He started and half-reached for an open drawer, intending a gun-play, undoubtedly, then bethought himself and growled:

" 'This is no bank.'

" 'Nor have I checks to cash. But I have, sir, an idea, which, by your leave and kind assistance, I shall transmute into cash. In short, how does a tramp sketch, done by a tramp to the life, strike you? Are you open to it? Do your readers hunger for it? Do they crave after it? Can they be happy without it?'

"I thought for a moment that he would have an apoplexy, but he quelled the unruly blood and said he liked my nerve. I thanked him and assured him I liked it myself. Then he offered me a cigar and said he thought he'd do business with me.

" 'But mind you,' he said, when he had jabbed a bunch of copy paper into my hand and given me a pencil from his vest pocket, 'mind you, I won't stand for the high and flightly philosophical, and I perceive you have a tendency that way. Throw in the local color, wads of it, and a bit of sentiment perhaps, but no slumgullion about political economy or social strata or such stuff. Make it concrete, to the point, with snap and go and life, crisp and crackling and interesting — tumble?'

"And I tumbled and borrowed a dollar.

" 'Don't forget the local color!' he shouted after me through the door.

"And, Anak, it was the local color that did for me.

"The anæmic Cerberus grinned when I took the elevator. 'Get the bounce, eh?'

" 'Nay, pale youth so lily-white,' I chortled, waving the copy paper; 'not the bounce, but a detail. I'll be city editor in three months, and then I'll make you jump.'

"And as the elevator boy stopped at the next floor down to take on a pair of maids, he strolled over to the shaft, and without frills or verbiage, consigned me and my detail to the deepest perdition. But I liked him. He had pluck and was unafraid, and he knew, as well as I, that Death clutched him close."

"But how could you, Leith," I cried, the picture of the consumptive lad strong before me, "how could you treat him so barbarously?"

Leith laughed dryly.

"My dear fellow, how often must I explain to you your confusions? Orthodox sentiment and stereotyped emotion master you. And then your temperament! You are really incapable of rational judgments. Cerberus? Pshaw! A flash expiring, a mote of fading sparkle, a dim-pulsing and dying organism — pouf! a snap of the fingers, a puff of breath, what would you? A pawn in the game of life. Not even a problem. There is no problem in a still-born babe, nor in a dead child. They never arrived. Nor did Cerberus. Now for a really pretty problem — "

"But the local color?" I prodded him.

"That's right," he replied. "Keep me in the running. Well, I took my handful of copy paper down to the railroad yards (for local color), dangled my legs from a side-door Pullman, which is another name for a box car; and ran off the stuff. Of course I made it clever and brilliant and all that, with my little unanswerable slings at the State and my social paradoxes, and withal made it concrete enough to dissatisfy the average citizen. From the tramp standpoint, the constabulary of the township was particularly rotten, and I proceeded to open the eyes of the good people. It is a proposition, mathematically demonstrable, that it costs the community more to arrest, convict and confine its tramps in jail than to send them as guests, for like periods of time, to a first-class hotel. And this I developed, giving the facts and figures, the constable fees and the mileage, and the court and jail expenses. Oh, it was convincing, and it was true; and I did it in a lightly humorous fashion which fetched the laugh and left the sting. The main objection to the system, I contended, was the defrauding and robbery of the tramp. The good money which the community paid out for him should enable him to riot in luxury instead of rotting in dungeons. I even drew the figures so fine as to permit him not only to live in a good hotel, but to smoke two twenty-five-cent cigars and indulge in a ten-cent shine each day, and still not cost the taxpayers so much as they were accustomed to pay for his conviction and jail entertainment. And, as subsequent events proved, it made the taxpayers wince.

"One of the constables I drew to the life; nor did I forget a certain Sol Glenhart, as rotten a police judge to be found between the seas. And this I say out of a vast experience. While he was notorious in local trampdom, his civic sins were not only not unknown, but a crying reproach to the townspeople. Of course,

I refrained from mentioning name or habitat, drawing the picture in an impersonal, composite sort of way, which none the less blinded no one to the faithfulness of the local color.

"Naturally, myself a tramp, the tenor of the article was a protest against the maltreatment of the tramp. Cutting the tax-payers to the pits of their purses threw them open to sentiment, and then in I tossed the sentiment, lumps and chunks of it. Trust me, it was excellently done, and the rhetoric — say! just listen ιο the tail of my peroration:

> " 'So, as we go *mooching* along the drag, with a sharp lamp out for John Law, we cannot help remembering that we are beyond the pale; that our ways are not their ways; and that the ways of John Law with us are different from his ways with other men. Poor lost souls wailing for a crust in the dark, we know full well our helplessness and ignominy. And well may we repeat after a stricken brother over-seas: "Our pride it is to know no spur of pride." Man has fogotten us; God has forgotten us; only are we remembered by the harpies of justice, who prey upon our distress and coin our sighs and tears into bright shining dollars.'

"Incidentally, my picture of Sol Glenhart, the police judge, was good. A striking likeness, and unmistakable, with phrases tripping along like this: 'This crook-nosed, gross-bodied harpie'; 'this civic sinner, this judicial highwayman'; 'possessing the morals of the Tenderloin and an honor which thieves' honor puts to shame'; who compounds criminality with shyster-sharks, and in atonement railroads the unfortunate and impecunious to rotting cells' — and so forth, and so forth, style sophomoric and devoid of the dignity and tone one would employ in a dissertation on 'Surplus Value' or 'The Fallacies of Marxism,' but just the stuff the dear public likes.

" 'Humph!' grunted Spargo when I put the copy in his fist. 'Swift gait you strike, my man.'

"I fixed an hypnotic eye on his vest pocket and he passed out one of his superior cigars, which I burned while he ran through the stuff. Twice or thrice he looked over the top of the paper at me, searchingly, but said nothing till he had finished.

" 'Where'd you work, you pencil-pusher?' he asked.

" 'My maiden effort,' I simpered, modestly, scraping one foot and faintly simulating embarrassment.

" 'Maiden hell! What salary do you want?'

" 'Nay, nay, I answered. 'No salary in mine, thank you most to death. I am a free downtrodden American citizen, and no man shall say my time is his.'

" 'Save John Law,' he chuckled.

" 'Save John Law,' said I.

" 'How did you know I was bucking the police department?' he demanded, abruptly.

" 'I didn't know, but I knew you were in training,' I answered. 'Yesterday morning a charitably inclined female presented me with three biscuits, a piece of cheese, and a funereal slab of chocolate cake, all wrapped in the current *Clarion, wherein* I noted an unholy glee because the *Cowbell's* candidate for chief of police had been turned down. Likewise I learned the municipal election was at hand, and put two and two together. Another mayor, and the right kind, means new police commissioners; new police commissioners means new chief of police; new chief of police means *Cowbell's* candidate; *ergo,* your turn to play.'

"He stood up, shook my hand, and emptied his plethoric vest pocket. I put them away and puffed on the old one.

" 'You'll do,' he jubilated. 'This stuff' (patting my copy) 'is the first gun of the campaign. You'll touch off many another before we're done. I've been looking for you for years. Come on in, on the editorial.'

"But I shook my head.

" 'Come, now!' he admonished, sharply. 'No shenanagin! The *Cowbell* must have you. It hungers for you, craves after you, won't be happy till it gets you. What say?"

"In short, he wrestled with me, but I was bricks, and at the end of half an hour the only Spargo gave it up.

" 'Remember,' he said, 'any time you reconsider, I'm open. No matter where you are, wire me and I'll send the ducats to come on at once.'

"I thanked him, and asked the pay for my copy — *dope,* he called it.

" 'Oh, regular routine,' he said. 'Get it the first Thursday after publication.'

" 'Then I'll have to trouble you for a few scads until — '

"He looked at me and smiled. 'Better cough up, eh?'

" 'Sure,' I said. 'Nobody to identify me, so make it cash.'

"And cash it was made, thirty *plunks* (a plunk is a dollar, my dear Anak), and I pulled my freight . . . eh? Oh, departed.

" 'Pale youth.' I said to Cerberus, 'I am bounced.' (He grinned with pallid joy.) 'And in token of the sincere esteem I bear you, receive this little' — his eyes flashed and he threw up one hand, swiftly, to guard his head from the expected blow — 'this little memento.'

"I had intended to slip a fiver into his hand, but for all his surprise, he was too quick for me.

" 'Aw, keep yer dirt,' he snarled.

" 'I like you still better,' I said, adding a second fiver. 'You grow perfect. But you must take it.'

"He backed away growling, but I caught him around the neck, roughed what little wind he had out of him, and left him doubled up with the two fives in his pocket. But hardly had the elevator started when the two coins tinkled on the roof and fell down between the car and the shaft. As luck had it, the door was not closed, and I put out my hand and caught them. The elevator boy's eyes bulged.

" 'It's a way I have,' I said, airily, pocketing them.

" 'Some bloke's dropped 'em down the shaft,' he whispered, visibly awed by the circumstance.

" 'It stands to reason,' said I.

" 'I'll take charge of 'em,' he volunteered.

" 'Nonsense!' "

"You'd bett'r turn' 'em over,' he threatened, 'or I stop the works.'

" 'Pshaw!'

"And stop he did, between floors.

" 'Young man,' I said, 'have you a mother?' (He looked serious, as though regretting his act, and to further impress him I rolled up my right sleeve with greatest care.) 'Are you prepared to die?' (I got a stealthy crouch on, and put a cat-foot forward.) 'But a minute, a brief minute, stands between you and eternity.' (Here I crooked my right hand into a claw and slid the other foot up.) 'Young man, young man,' I trumpeted, 'in thirty seconds I shall tear your heart dripping from your bosom and stoop to hear you shriek in hell.'

"It fetched him. He gave one whoop, the car shot down, and I was on the drag. You see, Anak, it's a habit I can't shake off of leaving vivid memories behind. No one ever forgets me.

"I had not got to the corner when I heard a familiar voice at my shoulder:

" 'Hello, Cinders! Which way?'

"It was Chi Slim, who had been with me once when I was thrown off a freight in Jacksonville. 'Couldn't see 'm fer cinders,' he described it, and the monica stuck by me. . . . Monica? From *monos*. The tramp nickname.

" 'Bound south,' I answered. 'And how's Slim?'

" 'Bum. Bulls is horstile.'

" 'Where's the push?'

" 'At the hang-out. I'll put you wise.'

" 'Who's the main guy?'

" 'Me, and don't yer forget it.' "

The lingo was rippling from Leith's lips, but perforce stopped him.

"Pray translate. Remember, I am a foreigner."

"Certainly," he answered, cheerfully. "Slim is in poor luck. *Bull* means policeman. He tells me the bulls are hostile. I ask where the *push* is, the gang he travels with. By *putting me wise* he will direct me to where the gang is hanging out. The *main guy* is the leader. Slim claims that distinction.

"Slim and I hiked out to a neck of woods just beyond town,

and there was the push, a score of husky hobos, charmingly located on the bank of a little purling stream.

" 'Come on, you mugs!' Slim addressed them. 'Throw yer feet! Here's Cinders, an' we must do 'm proud.'

"All of which signifies that the hobos had better strike out and do some lively begging in order to get the wherewithal to celebrate my return to the fold after a year's separation. But I flashed my dough and Slim sent several of the younger men off to buy the booze. Take my word for it; Anak, it was a blow-out memorable in Trampdom to this day. It's amazing the quantity of booze thirty plunks will buy, and it is equally amazing the quantity of booze twenty stiffs will get outside of. Beer and cheap wine made up the card, with alcohol thrown in for the *blowed-in-the-glass stiffs*. It was great — an orgy under the sky, a contest of beakermen, a study in primitive beastliness. To me there is something fascinating in a drunken man, and were I a college president I should institute P. G. psychology courses in practical drunkenness. It would beat the books and compete with the laboratory.

"All of which is neither here nor there, for after sixteen hours of it, early next morning, the whole push was *copped* by an overwhelming array of constables and carted off to jail. After breakfast, about ten o'clock, we were lined upstairs into court, limp and spiritless, the twenty of us. And there, under his purple panoply, nose crooked like a Napoleonic eagle and eyes glittering and beady, sat Sol Glenhart.

" 'John Ambrose!' the clerk called out, and Chi Slim, with the ease of long practice, stood up.

" 'Vagrant, your honor,' the bailiff volunteered, and his honor, not deigning to look at the prisoner, snapped: 'Ten days,' and Chi Slim sat down.

"And so it went, with the monotony of clockwork, fifteen seconds to the man, four men to the minute, the mugs bobbing up and down in turn like marionettes. The clerk called the name, the bailiff the offense, the judge the sentence, and the man sat down. That was all. Simple, eh? Superb!

"Chi Slim nudged me. 'Give 'm a *spiel,* Cinders. You kin do it.'

"I shook my head.

" 'G'wan,' he urged. 'Give 'm a ghost story. The mugs 'll take it all right. And you kin throw yer feet fer tobacco for us till we get out.'

" 'L. C. Randolph!' the clerk called.

"I stood up, but a hitch came in the proceedings. The clerk whispered to the judge, and the bailiff smiled.

" 'You are a newspaper man, I understand. Mr. Randolph?' his Honor remarked, sweetly.

"It took me by surprise, for I had forgotten the *Cowbell* in the excitement of succeeding events, and I now saw myself on the edge of the pit I had digged.

" 'That's yer *graft.* Work it,' Slim prompted.

" 'It's all over but the shouting.' I groaned back but Slim, unaware of the article, was puzzled.

" 'Your Honor,' I answered, 'when I can get work, that is my occupation.'

" 'You take quite an interest in local affairs, I see.' (Here his Honor took up the morning's *Cowbell* and ran his eye up and down a column I knew was mine.) 'Color is good,' he commented, an appreciative twinkle in his eye; 'pictures excellent, characterized by broad Sargent-like effects. Now this . . . this judge you have depicted . . . you, ah, draw from life, I presume?'

" 'Rarely, your Honor,' I answered. 'Composites, ideas, rather . . . er, I may say.'

" 'But you have color, sir, unmistakable color,' he continued.

" 'That is splashed on afterward,' I explained.

" 'This judge, then, is not modeled from life, as one might be led to believe?'

" 'No, your Honor.'

" 'Ah, I see, merely a type of judicial wickedness?'

" 'Nay, more, your Honor,' I said, boldly; 'an ideal.'

" 'Splashed with local color afterward? Ha! Good! And may I venture to ask how much you received for this bit of work?'

" 'Thirty dollars, your Honor.'

" 'Hum, good!' And his tone abruptly changed. 'Young man, local color is a bad thing. I find you guilty of it and sentence you to thirty days' imprisonment, or, at your pleasure, impose a fine of thirty dollars.'

" 'Alas!' said I. 'I spent the thirty dollars in riotous living.'

" 'And thirty days more for wasting your substance. Next case!' said his Honor to the clerk.

"Slim was stunned. 'Gee!' he whispered. 'Gee! The push gets ten days and you get sixty. Gee!'"

Leith struck a match, lighted his dead cigar and opened the book on his knees.

"Returning to the original conversation, don't you find, Anak, that though Loria handles the bi-partition of the revenues with scrupulous care, he yet omits one important factor, namely — "

"Yes," I said, absently; "yes."

"The Tramp"

Few of London's works traveled more widely than this essay before it found a home. Beginning with McClure's *in December of 1901, London tried twenty magazines — including* Century *(twice),* Cosmopolitan, Atlantic, Saturday Evening Post, Collier's Weekly, *and* Harper's Monthly — *before* Wilshire's *accepted the essay. Even after its acceptance London had difficulty getting paid for the essay. Gaylord Wilshire, the millionaire socialist, told London he could not afford to pay him even one cent per word for "The Tramp" and for London's book.* The People of the Abyss *(1903). Later, Wilshire sent London stock in payment for his writings, and he also reprinted "The Tramp" in booklet form in 1904 (Gaylord Wilshire to London, July 29, 1904, Box 63, JLP, HEH, "No. 2. Magazine Sales, From May 1900 to Feb. 1903," Box 19, JCLC, USU).*

Illustrative of the comments that London received from editors when they read "The Tramp" are the reactions of Bliss Perry, the editor of Atlantic: *"We have read the tramp essay over and over again, and have submitted it to two or three people without being able to convince ourselves finally that its general thesis is tenable." Perry to London, April 24, 1902, Box 46, JLP, HEH.*

Mr. Francis O'Neil, General Superintendent of Police, Chicago, speaking of the tramps, says:* "Despite the most stringent police regulations, a great city will have a certain number of homeless vagrants to shelter through the winter." *"Despite"* — mark the word — a confession of organized helplessness as against unorganized necessity. If police regulations are stringent and yet fail, then

---

Source: *The Tramp.* Chicago: Charles H. Kerr and Company, 1904.
*The Saturday Evening Post, Nov. 23, 1904.

that which makes them fail, namely, the tramp, must have still more stringent reasons for succeeding. This being so, it should be of interest to enquire into these reasons, to attempt to discover why the nameless and homeless vagrant sets at naught the right arm of the corporate power of our great cities, why all that is weak and worthless is stronger than all that is strong and of value.

Mr. O'Neil is a man of wide experience on the subject of tramps. He may be called a specialist. As he says of himself: "As an old-time desk sergeant and police captain, I have had almost unlimited opportunity to study and analyze this class of floating population which seeks the city in winter and scatters abroad through the country in the spring." He then continues:

"This experience reiterated the lesson that the vast majority of these wanderers are of the class with whom a life of vagrancy is a chosen means of living without work." Not only is it to be inferred from this that there is a large class in society which lives without work, for Mr. O'Neil's testimony further shows that this class is *forced* to live without work.

As he says: "I have been astonished at the multitude of those who have unfortunately engaged in occupations which practically force them to become loafers for at least a third of the year. And it is from this class that the tramps are largely recruited. I recall a certain winter when it seemed to me that a large portion of the inhabitants of Chicago belonged to this army of unfortunates. I was stationed at a police station not far from where an ice harvest was ready for the cutters. The ice company advertised for helpers, and the very night this call appeared in the newspapers our station was packed with homeless men who asked for shelter in order to be at hand for the morning's work. Every foot of floor space was given over to these lodgers and scores were still unaccommodated."

And again: "And it must be confessed that the man who is willing to do honest labor for food and shelter is a rare specimen in this vast army of shabby and tattered wanderers who seek the warmth of the city with the coming of the first snow." Taking into consideration the crowd of honest laborers that swamped Mr. O'Neil's station house on the way to the ice-cutting, it is patent, if all tramps were looking for honest labor instead of a small minority, that the honest laborers would have a far harder task finding something honest to do for food and shelter. If the opinion of the honest laborers who swamped Mr. O'Neil's station house were asked one could rest confident that each and every man would express a preference for fewer honest laborers on the morrow when he asked the ice-foreman for a job.

And finally, Mr. O'Neil says: "The humane and generous treatment which this city has accorded the great army of homeless unfortunates has made it the victim of wholesale imposition, and this well-intended policy of kindness has resulted in making Chicago the winter Mecca of a vast and undesirable floating population." That is to say, because of her kindness, Chicago had more than her fair share of tramps; because she was humane and generous she suffered wholesale imposition. From this we must conclude that it does not do to be *humane* and *generous* to our fellow men . . . when they are tramps. Mr. O'Neil is right, and that this is no sophism it is the intention of this article, among other things, to prove.

In a general way we may draw the following inferences from the remarks of Mr. O'Neil: (1) The tramp is stronger than organized society and cannot be put down. (2) The tramp is "shabby," "tattered," homeless," "unfortunate." (3) There are a "vast" number of tramps. (4) Very few tramps are willing to do honest work. (5) Those tramps who are willing to do honest work have to hunt very hard to find it. (6) The tramp is undesirable.

To this latter let the contention be appended that the tramp is only *personally* undesirable; that he is *negatively* desirable; that the function he performs in society is a negative function; and that he is the by-product of economic necessity.

It is very easy to demonstrate that there are more men than there is work for men. For instance, what would happen tomorrow if one hundred thousand tramps should become suddenly inspired with an overmastering desire for work? It is a fair question. "Go to work" is preached to the tramp every day of his life. The judge on the bench, the pedestrian in the street, the housewife at the kitchen door, all unite in advising him to go to work. So, what would happen tomorrow if one hundred thousands tramps acted upon this advice and strenuously and indomitably sought work? Why, by the end of the week one hundred thousand workers, their places taken by the tramps, would receive their time and be "hitting the road" for a job.

Ella Wheeler Wilcox unwittingly and uncomfortably demonstrated the disparity between men and work. She made a casual reference, in a newspaper column she conducts, to the difficulty two business men found in obtaining good employees. The first morning mail brought her seventy-five applications for the position and at the end of two weeks over two hundred people had applied.

Still more striking was the same proposition demonstrated this past summer in San Francisco. A sympathetic strike called out a whole federation of trades unions. Thousands of men, in many branches of trade, quit work — draymen, sand teamsters, porters and packers, longshoremen, stevedores, warehousemen, stationary engineers, sailors, marine firemen, stewards, sea cooks, and so forth and so forth, an interminable list. It was a strike of large proportions. Every Pacific coast shipping city was involved, and the entire coasting service from San Diego to Puget Sound was virtually tied up. The time was considered auspicious. The Philippines and Alaska had drained the Pacific coast of surplus labor. It was summertime, when the agricultural demand for laborers was at its height, and when the cities were bare of their floating populations. And yet there remained a body of surplus labor sufficient to take the places of the strikers. No matter what occupation — sea cook or stationary engineer, sand teamster or warehouseman — in every case there was an idle worker ready to do the work. And not only ready, but anxious. They fought for a chance to work. Men were killed, hundreds of heads were broken, the hospitals were filled with injured men, and thousands of assaults were committed. And still surplus laborers, "scabs," came forward to replace the strikers.

The question arises: *Whence came this second army of workers to replace the first army?* One thing is certain: the trades unions did not scab on one another. Another thing is certain: no industry on the Pacific slope was crippled in the slightest degree by its workers being drawn away to fill the places of the strikers. A third thing is certain: the agricultural workers did not flock to the cities to replace the strikers. In this last instance it is worth while to note that the agricultural laborers wailed to high heaven when a few of the strikers went into the country to compete with them in un-skilled employments. So there is no accounting for this second army of workers. It simply was. It was there all the time, a surplus labor army in that year of Our Lord, 1903, a year adjudged most prosperous in the annals of the United States.

And this particular strike is analogous to all other strikes. Always, no matter what or where the strike, or how far-reaching, always have the tools dropped by one set of men been taken up by another set of men.

THE SURPLUS LABOR ARMY.

The existence of the surplus labor army being established, there remains to be established the economic necessity for the surplus labor army. The simplest and most obvious need is that brought about by the fluctuation of production. If, when produc-tion is at low ebb, all men are at work, it necessarily follows that when production increases there will be no men to do the increased work. This may seem almost childish and if not childish, at least easily remedied. At low-ebb let the men work shorter time; at high-flood let them work over-time. The main objection to this is that it is not done, and that we are considering what is, not what might be or should be.

Then there are great irregular and periodical demands for labor which must be met. Under the first head come all the big building and engineering enterprises. When a canal is to be dug, or a railroad put through, requiring thousands of laborers, it would be hurtful to withdraw these laborers from the constant industries. And whether it is a canal to be dug or a cellar, whether five thousand men are required or five, it is well, in society as at present organized, that they be taken from the surplus labor army. The surplus labor army is the reserve fund of social energy, and this is one of the reasons for its existence.

Under the second head, periodical demands, come the harvests. Throughout the year huge labor tides sweep back and forth across the United States. That which is sown and tended by few men, comes to sudden ripeness and must be gathered by many men; and it is inevitable that these many men form floating populations. In the late spring the berries must be picked, and in the summer the grain garnered, in the fall the hops gathered, in the winter the ice harvested. In California a man may pick berries in Siskiyou, peaches in Santa Clara, grapes in San Joaquin, and oranges in Los Angeles, going from job to job as the season advances and traveling a thousand miles ere the season is done. But the great demand for agricultural labor is in the summer. In the winter, work is slack, and these floating populations eddy into the cities to eke out a precarious existence and harrow the souls of the police officers until the return of warm weather and work. If there were constant work at good wages for every man, who else would harvest the crops? And society, after the centuries, cannot say who else.

THE LASH OF THE MASTER.

But the last and most significant need for the surplus labor army remains to be stated: This surplus labor acts as a check upon all employed labor. It is the lash by which the masters hold the workers to their tasks or drive them back to their tasks when they have revolted. It is the goad which forces the workers into the compulsory "free contracts" against which they now and again rebel. There is only one reason under the sun that strikes fail, and that is because there are always plenty of men to take the strikers' places. This is indisputable.

The strength of the union today, other things remaining equal, is proportionate to the skill of the trade, or, in other words, proportionate to the pressure the surplus labor army can put upon it. If a thousand ditch-diggers strike it is easy to replace them, wherefore the ditch-diggers have little or no organized strength. But a thousand highly skilled machinists are somewhat harder to replace, and in consequence the machinist unions are strong. The ditch-diggers are wholly at the mercy of the surplus labor army, the machinists only partly. To be invincible, a union must be a monopoly. It must control every man in its particular trade and regulate apprentices so that the supply of skilled workmen remain constant — this is the dream of the "Labor Trust" on the part of the captains of labor.

Once, in England, after the Great Plague, labor awoke to find there was more work for men than there were men to work. Instead of workers competing for favors from employers, employers were competing for favors from the workers. Wages went up, and up, and continued to go up, until the workers demanded the full product of their toil. Now it is clear that when labor receives its full product capital must perish. And so the pigmy capitalists of that post-Plague day found their existence threatened by this untoward condition of affairs. To save themselves they set a maximum wage, restrained the workers from moving about from place to place, smashed incipient organization, refused to tolerate idlers, and by most barbarous legal penalties punished those who disobeyed. After that, things went on as before.

THE ANCHOR OF CAPITALISM.

The point of this, of course, is to demonstrate the need of the surplus labor army. Without such an army our present capitalist society would be powerless. Labor would organize as it never organized before, and the last least worker would be gathered into the unions. The full product of toil would be demanded, and capitalist society would crumble away. Nor could capitalist society save itself as did the post-Plague capitalist society. The time is past when a handful of masters, by imprisonment and barbarous punishment, can drive the legions of the workers to their tasks. Without a surplus labor army, the courts, police and military are impotent. In such matters the function of the courts, police and military is to preserve order and fill the places of strikers with surplus labor. If there be no surplus labor to instate, there is no function; for disorder only arises during the process of instatement when the striking labor army and the surplus labor army clash together. That is to say, that which subserves the integrity of the present industrial society more potently than the courts, police and military, is the surplus labor army.

It has been shown that there are more men than there is work for men, and that the surplus labor army is an economic necessity. To show how the tramp is a by-product of this economic necessity, it is necessary to inquire into the composition of the surplus labor army. What men form it? Why are they there? What do they do?

THE INEFFICIENTS.

In the first place, since the workers must compete for employment, it inevitably follows that it is the fit and efficient who find employment. The skilled worker holds his place by virtue of his skill and efficiency. Were he less skilled, or were he unreliable or erratic, he would be swiftly replaced by a stronger competitor. The skilled and steady employments are not cumbered with clowns and idiots. A man finds his place according to his ability and the needs of the system, and those without ability or incapable of satisfying the needs of the system, have no place. Thus, the poor telegrapher may develop into an excellent woodchopper. But if the poor telegrapher cherishes the delusion that he is a good telegrapher, and at the same time disdains all other employments, he will have no employment at all, or he will be so poor at all other employments that he will work only now and again in lieu of better men. He will be among the first let off when times are dull, and among the last taken on when times are good. Or, to the point, he will be a member of the surplus labor army.

So the conclusion is reached that the less fit and less efficient, or the unfit and inefficient, compose the surplus labor army. Here are to be found the men who have tried and failed, the men who cannot hold jobs — the plumber apprentice who could not become a journeyman, and the plumber journeyman too clumsy and dull to retain employment; switchmen who throw trains, clerks who cannot balance books, blacksmiths who lame horses, lawyers who cannot plead; in short, the failures of every trade and profession, and failures many of them in divers trades and professions. Failure is writ large, and in their wretchedness they bear the stamp of social disapprobation. Common work, any kind of work, wherever or however they can obtain it, is their portion.

But these hereditary inefficients do not alone compose the

surplus labor army. There are the skilled but unsteady and unreliable men, and the old men, once skilled but, with dwindling life, no longer skilled. And there are good men, too, splendidly skilled and efficient, but thrust out of employment of dying or disaster-smitten industries. In this connection it is not out of place to note the misfortune of the workers in the British iron trades who are suffering because of American inroads. And last of all, are the unskilled laborers, the hewers of wood and drawers of water, the ditch-diggers, the men of pick and shovel, the helpers, lumpers, roustabouts. If trade is slack on a seacoast of two thousand miles, or the harvest light in a great interior valley, myriads of these laborers lie idle or make life miserable for their fellows in kindred unskilled employments.

A constant filtration goes on in the working world, and good material is continually drawn from the surplus labor army. Strikes and industrial dislocations shake up the workers, fetch good men to the surface and sink men not so good. After the Pullman strike a few thousand railroad men were chagrined to find the work they had flung down taken up by men as good as themselves.

But one thing must be considered here. Under the present system, if the weakest and least fit were as strong and fit as the best, and were the best proportionately stronger and fitter, the same condition would obtain. There would be the same army of unemployed labor, the same army of surplus labor. The whole thing is relative. There is no absolute standard of efficiency.

THE TRAMP NECESSARY.

Comes now the tramp. And all conclusions may be anticipated by saying at once that he is a tramp because some one had to be a tramp. If he left the "road" and became a *very* efficient common laborer, some *ordinary* efficient common laborer would have to take to the "road." The nooks and crannies are crowded by the surplus laborers, and when the first snow flies and the tramps are driven into the cities, things become overcrowded and stringent police regulations are necessary.

The tramp is one of two kinds of men: he is either a discouraged worker or a discouraged criminal. Now a discouraged criminal, on investigation, proves to be a discouraged worker or a descendant of discouraged workers; so that in the last analysis the tramp is a discouraged worker. Since there is not work for all, discouragement for some is unavoidable. How, then, does this process of discouragement operate?

The lower the employment in the industrial scale, the harder the conditions. The finer, the more delicate, the more skilled the trade, the higher it is lifted above the struggle. There is less pressure, less sordidness, less savagery. There are fewer glass blowers proportionate to the needs of the glass-blowing industry than there are ditch-diggers to the ditch-digging industry. And not only this, for it requires a glass blower to take the place of a striking glass blower, while any kind of a striker or out-of-work can take the place of a ditch-digger. So the skilled trades are more independent, have more individuality and latitude. They may confer with their masters, make demands, assert themselves. The unskilled laborers, on the other hand, have no voice in their affairs. The settlement of terms is none of their business. "Free contract" is all that remains to them. They may take what is offered or leave it. There are plenty more of their kind. They do not count. They are members of the surplus labor army and must be content with a hand to mouth existence.

The reward is likewise proportioned. The strong, fit worker in a skilled trade, where there is little labor pressure, is well compensated. He is a king compared with his less fortunate brothers in the unskilled occupations where the labor pressure is great. The mediocre worker not only is forced to be idle a large portion of the time, but when employed is forced to accept a pittance. A dollar a day on some days and nothing on others will hardly support a man and wife and send children to school. And not only do the masters bear heavily upon him, and his own kind struggle for the morsel at his mouth, but all skilled and organized labor adds to his woe. Union men do not scab on one another, but in strikes or when work is slack it is considered "fair" for them to descend and take away the work of the common laborers. And take it away they do, for, as a matter of fact, a well-fed, ambitious machinist or coremaker will transiently shovel coal better than an ill-fed, spirit-less laborer.

Thus there is no encouragement for the unfit, inefficient and mediocre. Their very inefficiency and mediocrity make them help-less as cattle and add to their misery. And the whole tendency for such is downward, until, at the bottom of the society pit, they are wretched, inarticulate beasts, living like beasts, breeding like beasts, dying like beasts. And how do they fare, these creatures born mediocre, where heritage is neither brains nor brawn nor endur-ance? They are sweated in the slums in an atmosphere of discour-agement and despair. There is no strength in weakness, no encouragement in foul air, vile food, and dank dens. They are there because they are so made that they are not fit to be higher up; but filth and obscenity do not strengthen the neck, nor does chronic emptiness of belly stiffen the back.

For the mediocre there is no hope. Mediocrity is a sin. Poverty is the penalty of failure — poverty, from whose loins spring the criminal and the tramp, both failures, both discouraged work-ers. Poverty is the inferno where ignorance festers and vice cor-rodes, and where the physical, mental and moral parts of human nature are aborted and denied.

DETAILS OF THE PICTURE.

That the charge of rashness in splashing the picture be not incurred, let the following authoritative evidence be considered: First, the work and wages of mediocrity and inefficiency, and second, the habits.

The New York Sun of February 28, 1901, describes the open-ing of a factory in New York City by the American Tobacco Com-pany. Cheroots were to be made in this factory in competition with other factories which refused to be absorbed by the trust. The trust advertised for girls. The crowd of men and boys who wanted work was so great in front of the building that the police were forced with their clubs to clear them away. The wage paid the girls was $2.50 per week, sixty cents of which went for car fare.

Miss Nellie Mason Auten, a graduate student of the depart-ment of sociology at the University of Chicago, recently made a thorough investigation of the garment trades of Chicago. Her figures were published in the *American Journal of Sociology* and commented upon by the *Literary Digest*. She found women working ten hours a day, six days a week, for forty cents per week (a rate of two-thirds of a cent an hour). Many women earned less than a dollar a week, and none of them worked every week. The following table will best summarize Miss Auten's investigations among a portion of the garment workers:

	Average Individual weekly wages.	Average Number of weeks employed.	Average yearly earnings.
Dressmakers	$ .90	42.	$37.00
Pants finishers	1.31	27.58	42.41
Housewives and pant finishers	1.58	30.21	47.49
Seamstresses	2.03	32.78	64.10
Pants makers	2.13	30.77	75.61
Miscellaneous	2.77	29.	81.80
Tailors	6.22	31.96	211.92
General average	$2.48	31.18	$76.74

Walter A. Wyckoff, who is as great an authority upon the worker as Josiah Flynt is on the tramp, furnishes the following Chicago experience:

"Many of the men were so weakened by the want and hardship of the winter that they were no longer in condition for effective labor. Some of the bosses who were in need of added hands were obliged to turn men away because of physical incapacity. One instance of this I shall not soon forget. It was when I overheard, early one morning, at a factory gate, an interview between a would-be laborer and the boss. I knew the applicant for a Russian-Jew, who had at home an old mother and a wife and two young children to support. He had had intermittent employment throughout the winter in a sweater's den, barely enough to keep them all alive, and, after the hardships of the cold season, he was again in desperate straits for work.

"The boss had all but agreed to take him on for some sort of unskilled labor, when, struck by the cadaverous look of the man, he told him to bare his arm. Up went the sleeve of his coat and his ragged flannel shirt, exposing a naked arm with the muscles nearly gone, and the blue-white transparent skin stretched over sinews and the outline of the bones. Pitiful beyond words were his efforts to give a semblance of strength to the biceps which rose faintly to the upward movement of the forearm. But the boss sent him off with an oath and a contemptuous laugh, and I watched the fellow as he turned down the street, facing the fact of his starving family with a despair at his heart which only mortal man can feel and no mortal tongue can speak."

Concerning habitat, Mr. Jacob Riis states that in New York City in the block bounded by Stanton, Houston, Attorney and Ridge streets, the size of which is 200x300, there is a warren of 2,244 human beings.

In the block bounded by Sixty-first and Sixty-second streets, and Amsterdam and West End avenues, are over four thousand human creatures — quite a comfortable New England village to crowd into one city block.

The Rev. Dr. Behrends, speaking of the block bounded by Canal, Hester, Eldridge and Forsyth streets, says: "In a room 12x8 and 5½ feet high, it was found that nine persons slept and prepared their food. . . . In another room, located in a dark cellar, without screens or partitions, were together, two men with their wives and a girl of fourteen, two single men and a boy of seventeen, two women and four boys — nine, ten, eleven and fifteen years old — fourteen persons in all."

Here humanity rots. Its victims, with grim humor, call it "Tenement-House Rot." Or, as a legislative report puts it: "Here infantile life unfolds its bud, but perishes before its first anniversary. Here youth is ugly with loathsome disease and the deformities which follow physical degeneration."

THE CALL OF THE "ROAD."

These are the men and women who are what they are because they are not better born, or because they happen to be unluckily born in time and space. Gauged by the needs of the system, they are weak and worthless. The hospital and the pauper's grave await them, and they offer no encouragement to the mediocre worker who has failed higher up in the industrial fabric. Such a worker, conscious that he has failed, conscious from the hard fact that he cannot obtain work in the higher employments, finds several courses open to him. He may come down and be a beast in the social pit, for instance; but if he be of a certain calibre, the effect of the social pit will be to discourage him from work. In his blood a rebellion will quicken, and he will elect to become either a felon or a tramp.

If he has fought the hard fight, he is not unacquainted with the lure of the "road." When out of work and still undiscouraged, he has been forced to "hit the road" between large cities in his quest for a job. He has loafed, seen the country and green things, laughed in joy, laid on his back and listened to the birds singing overhead, unannoyed by factory whistles and bosses' harsh commands; and, most significant of all, *he has lived.* That is the point! Not only has he been care-free and happy, but he has lived! And from the knowledge that he has idled and is still alive, he achieves a new outlook on life; and the more he experiences the unenviable lot of the poor worker, the more the blandishments of the "road" take hold of him. And finally he flings his challenge in the face of society, imposes a valorous boycott on all work, and joins the far-wanderers of Hobo-land, the gypsy-folk of this latter day.

But the tramp does not usually come from the slums. His place of birth is ordinarily a bit above, and sometimes a very great bit above. A confessed failure, he yet refuses to accept the punishment and swerves aside from the slum to vagabondage. The average beast in the social pit is either too much of a beast, or too much of a slave to the orthodox ethics and ideals of his masters, to manifest this flicker of rebellion. But the social pit, out of its discouragement and viciousness, breeds criminals, men who prefer to be beasts of prey over being beasts of work. And the mediocre criminal, in turn, the unfit and inefficient criminal, is discouraged by the strong arm of the law and goes over to trampdom.

These men, the discouraged worker and the discouraged criminal, voluntarily withdraw themselves from the struggle for work. Industry does not need them. There are no factories shut down through lack of labor, no projected railroads unbuilt for want of pick and shovel men. Women are still glad to toil for a dollar a week, and men and boys to clamor and fight for work at the factory gates. No one misses these discouraged men, and in going away they have made it somewhat easier for those that remain.

CONCLUSIONS.

So the case stands thus: There being more men than there is work for men, a surplus labor army inevitably results. The surplus labor army is an economic necessity; without it the present construction of society would fall to pieces. Into the surplus labor army are herded the mediocre, the inefficient, the unfit, and those incapable of satisfying the industrial needs of the system. The struggle for work between the members of the surplus labor army is sordid and savage, and at the bottom of the social pit the struggle is vicious and beastly. This struggle tends to discouragement, and the victims of this discouragement are the criminal and the tramp. The tramp is not an economic necessity such as the surplus labor army, but he is the by-product of an economic necessity.

The "road" is one of the safety valves through which the waste of the social organism is given off. And *being given off* constitutes the negative function of the tramp. Society, as at present organized, makes much waste of human life. This waste must be eliminated. Chloroform or electrocution would be a simple, merciful solution of this problem of elimination; but the ruling ethics, while permitting the human waste, will not permit a humane elimination of that waste. This paradox demonstrates the irreconcilability of theoretical ethics and industrial need.

And so the tramp becomes self-eliminating. And not only self! Since he is manifestly unfit for things as they are, and since kind is prone to beget kind, it is necessary that his kind cease with him, that his progeny shall not be, that he play the eunuch's part in this twentieth century after Christ. And he plays it. He does not breed. Sterility is his portion, as it is the portion of the woman on the street. They might have been mates, but society has decreed otherwise.

And while it is not nice that these men should die, it is ordained that they must die, and we should not quarrel with them if they cumber our highways and kitchen stoops with their perambulating carcasses. This is a form of elimination we not only countenance but compel. Therefore let us be cheerful and honest about it. Let us be as stringent as we please with our police regulations, but for goodness' sake let us refrain from telling the tramp to go to work. Not only is it unkind, but it is untrue and hypocritical. We know there is no work for him. And though we may not know, we should know that it is our duty to know, that he is, in a way, a hero. As the scapegoat to our economic and industrial sinning, or to the plan of things, if you will, we should give him credit. Let us be just. He is so made. Society made him. He did not make himself.

"What Life Means to Me"

I was born in the working class. I early discovered enthusiasm, ambition, and ideals; and to satisfy these became the problem of my childlife. My environment was crude and rough and raw. I had no outlook, but an uplook rather. My place in society was at the bottom. Here life offered nothing but sordidness and wretchedness, both of the flesh and the spirit; for here flesh and spirit were alike starved and tormented.

Above me towered the colossal edifice of society, and to my mind the only way out was up. Into this edifice I early resolved to climb. Up above, men wore black clothes and boiled shirts, and women dressed in beautiful gowns. Also, there were good things to eat, and there was plenty to eat. This much for the flesh. Then there were the things of the spirit. Up above me, I knew, were unselfishnesses of the spirit, clean and noble thinking, keen intellectual living. I knew all this because I read "Seaside Library" novels, in which, with the exception of the villains and adventuresses, all men and women thought beautiful thoughts, spoke a beautiful tongue, and performed glorious deeds. In short, as I accepted the rising of the sun, I accepted that up above me was all that was fine and noble and gracious, all that gave decency and dignity to life, all that made life worth living and that remunerated one for his travail and misery.

But it is not particularly easy for one to climb up out of the working class — especially if he is handicapped by the possession of ideals and illusions. I lived on a ranch in California, and I was hard put to find the ladder whereby to climb. I early inquired the

Source: *Cosmopolitan Magazine*, XL (March 1906), 526-530.

rate of interest on invested money, and worried my child's brain into an understanding of the virtues and excellencies of that remarkable invention of man, compound interest. Further, I ascertained the current rates of wages for workers of all ages, and the cost of living. From all this data I concluded that if I began immediately and worked and saved until I was fifty years of age, I could then stop working and enter into participation in a fair portion of the delights and goodnesses that would then be open to me higher up in society. Of course, I resolutely determined not to marry, while I quite forgot to consider at all that great rock of disaster in the working class world — sickness.

But the life that was in me demanded more than a meager existence of scraping and scrimping. Also, at ten years of age, I became a newsboy on the streets of a city, and found myself with a changed uplook. All about me were still the same sordidness and wretchedness, and up above me was still the same paradise waiting to be gained; but the ladder whereby to climb was a different one. It was now the ladder of business. Why save my earnings and invest in government bonds, when, by buying two newspapers for five cents, with a turn of the wrist I could sell them for ten cents and double my capital? The business ladder was the ladder for me, and I had a vision of myself becoming a baldheaded and successful merchant prince.

Alas for visions! When I was sixteen I had already earned the title of "prince." But this title was given me by a gang of cutthroats and thieves, by whom I was called "The Prince of the Oyster Pirates." And at that time I had climbed the first rung of the business ladder. I was a capitalist. I owned a boat and a complete oyster-pirating outfit. I had begun to exploit my fellow-creatures. I had a crew of one man. As captain and owner I took two thirds of the spoils, and gave the crew one-third, though the crew worked just as hard as I did and risked just as much his life and liberty.

This one rung was the heights I climbed up the business ladder. One night I went on a raid amongst the Chinese fishermen. Ropes and nets were worth dollars and cents. It was robbery, I grant, but it was precisely the spirit of capitalism. The capitalist takes away the possessions of his fellow-creatures by means of a rebate, or of a betrayal of trust, or by the purchase of senators and supreme-court judges. I was merely crude. That was the only difference. I used a gun.

But my crew that night was one of those inefficients against whom the capitalist is wont to fulminate, because, forsooth, such inefficients increase expenses and reduce dividends. My crew did both. What of his carelessness he set fire to the big mainsail and totally destroyed it. There weren't any dividends that night, and the Chinese fishermen were richer by the nets and ropes we did not get. I was bankrupt, unable just then to pay sixty-five dollars for a new mainsail. I left my boat at anchor and went off on a bay-pirate boat on a raid up the Sacramento River. While away on this trip, another gang of bay pirates raided my boat. They stole everything, even the anchors; and later on, when I recovered the drifting hulk, I sold it for twenty dollars. I had slipped back the one rung I had climbed, and never again did I attempt the business ladder.

From then on I was mercilessly exploited by other capitalists. I had the muscle, and they made money out of it while I made but a very indifferent living out of it. I was a sailor before the mast, a longshoreman, a roustabout; I worked in canneries, and factories, and laundries; I mowed lawns, and cleaned carpets, and washed windows. And I never got the full product of my toil. I looked at the daughter of the cannery owner, in her carriage, and knew that it was my muscle, in part, that helped drag along that carriage on its rubber tires. I looked at the son of the factory owner, going to college, and knew that it was my muscle that helped, in part, to pay for the wine and goodfellowship he enjoyed.

But I did not resent this. It was all in the game. They were the strong. Very well, I was strong. I would carve my way to a place amongst them, and make money out of the muscles of other men. I was not afraid of work. I loved hard work. I would pitch in and work harder than ever and eventually become a pillar of society.

And just then, as luck would have it, I found an employer that was of the same mind. I was willing to work, and he was more than willing that I should work. I thought I was learning a trade. In reality, I had displaced two men. I thought he was making an electrician out of me; as a matter of fact, he was making fifty dollars per month out of me. The two men I had displaced had received forty dollars each per month; I was doing the work of both for thirty dollars per month.

This employer worked me nearly to death. A man may love oysters, but too many oysters will disincline him toward that particular diet. And so with me. Too much work sickened me. I did not wish ever to see work again. I fled from work. I became a tramp, begging my way from door to door, wandering over the United States and sweating bloody sweats in slums and prisons.

I had been born in the working class, and I was now, at the age of eighteen, beneath the point at which I had started. I was down in the cellar of society, down in the subterranean depths of misery about which it is neither nice nor proper to speak. I was in the pit, the abyss, the human cesspool, the shambles and the charnel house of our civilization. This is the part of the edifice of society that society chooses to ignore. Lack of space compels me here to ignore it, and I shall say only that the things I there saw gave me a terrible scare.

I was scared into thinking I saw the naked simplicities of the complicated civilization in which I lived. Life was a matter of food and shelter. In order to get food and shelter men sold things. The merchant sold shoes, the politician sold his manhood, and the representative of the people, with exceptions, of course, sold his trust; while nearly all sold their honor. Women, too, whether on the street or in the holy bond of wedlock, were prone to sell their flesh. All things were commodities, all people bought and sold. The one commodity that labor had to sell was muscle. The honor of labor had no price in the market place. Labor had muscle, and muscle alone, to sell.

But there was a difference, a vital difference. Shoes and trust and honor had a way of renewing themselves. They were imperishable stocks. Muscle, on the other hand, did not renew. As the shoe merchant sold shoes, he continued to replenish his stock.

But there was no way of replenishing the laborer's stock of muscle. The more he sold of his muscle, the less of it remained to him. It was his one commodity, and each day his stock of it diminished. In the end, if he did not die before, he sold out and put up his shutters. He was a muscle bankrupt, and nothing remained to him but to go down into the cellar of society and perish miserably.

I learned, further, that brain was likewise a commodity. It, too, was different from muscle. A brain seller was only at his prime when he was fifty or sixty years old, and his wares were fetching higher prices than ever. But a laborer was worked out or broken down at forty-five or fifty. I had been in the cellar of society, and I did not like the place as a habitation. The pipes and drains were unsanitary, and the air was bad to breathe. If I could not live on the parlor floor of society, I could, at any rate, have a try at the attic. It was true, the diet there was slim, but the air at least was pure. So I resolved to sell no more muscle, and to become a vender of brains.

Then begain a frantic pursuit of knowledge. I returned to California and opened the books. While thus equipping myself to become a brain merchant, it was inevitable that I should delve into sociology. There I found, in a certain class of books, scientifically formulated, the simple sociological concepts I had already worked out for myself. Other and greater minds, before I was born, had worked out all that I had thought and a vast deal more. I discovered that I was a socialist.

The socialists were revolutionists, inasmuch as they struggled to overthrow the society of the present, and out of the material to build the society of the future. I, too, was a socialist and a revolutionist. I joined the groups of working-class and intellectual revolutionists, and for the first time came into intellectual living. Here I found keen-flashing intellects and brilliant wits; for here I met strong and alert-brained, withal horny-handed, members of the working class; unfrocked preachers too wide in their Christianity for any congregation of Mammon-worshipers; professors broken on the wheel of university subservience to the ruling class and flung out because they were quick with knowledge which they strove to apply to the affairs of mankind.

Here I found, also, warm faith in the human, glowing idealism, sweetnesses of unselfishness, reunciation and martyrdom — all the splendid, stinging things of the spirit. Here life was clean, noble, and alive. Here life rehabilitated itself, became wonderful and glorious; and I was glad to be alive. I was in touch with great souls who exalted flesh and spirit over dollars and cents; and to whom the thin wail of the starved slum-child meant more than all the pomp and circumstance of commercial expansion and world-empire. All about me were nobleness of purpose and heroism of effort, and my days and nights were sunshine and starshine, all fire and dew, with before my eyes, ever burning and blazing, the Holy Grail, Christ's own Grail, the warm human, long suffering and mal-treated, but to be rescued and saved at the last.

And I, poor foolish I, deemed all this to be a mere foretaste of the delights of living I should find higher above me in society. I had lost many illusions since the day I read "Seaside Library" novels on the California ranch. I was destined to lose many of the illusions I still retained.

As a brain merchant I was a success. Society opened its portals to me. I entered right in on the parlor floor, and my disillusionment proceeded rapidly. I sat down to dinner with the masters of society, and with the wives and daughters of the masters of society. The women were gowned beautifully, I admit; but to my naïve surprise I discovered that they were of the same clay as all the rest of the women I had known down below in the cellar. "The colonel's lady and Judy O'Grady were sisters under their skins" — and gowns.

It was not this, however, so much as their materialism, that shocked me. It is true these beautifully gowned, beautiful women prattled sweet little ideals and dear little moralities; but in spite of their prattle the dominant key of the life they lived was materialistic. And they were so sentimentally selfish! They assisted in all kinds of sweet little charities, and informed one of the fact, while all the time the food they ate and the beautiful clothes they wore were bought out of dividends stained with the blood of child labor, and sweated labor, and of prostitution itself. When I mentioned such facts, expecting in my innocence that these sisters of Judy O'Grady would at once strip off their blood-dyed silks and jewels, they became excited and angry, and read me preachments about the lack of thrift, the drink, and the innate depravity that caused all the misery in society's cellar. When I mentioned that I couldn't quite see that it was the lack of thrift, the intemperance and the depravity of a half-starved child of six that made it work twelve hours every night in a Southern cotton mill, these sisters of Judy O'Grady attacked my private life and called me an "agitator" — as though that, forsooth, settled the argument.

Nor did I fare better with the masters themselves. I had expected to find men who were clean, noble, and alive, whose ideals were clean, noble, and alive. I went about amongst the men who sat in the high places, the preachers, the politicians, the business men, the professors, and the editors. I ate meat with them, drank wine with them, automobiled with them, and studied them. It is true, I found many that were clean and noble; but with rare exceptions, they were not *alive*. I do verily believe I could count the exceptions on the fingers of my two hands. Where they were not alive with rottenness, quick with unclean life, they were merely the unburied dead — clean and noble, like well-preserved mummies, but not alive. In this connection I may especially mention the professors I met, the men who live up to that decadent university ideal, "the passionless pursuit of passionless intelligence."

I met men who invoked the name of the Prince of Peace in their diatribes against war, and put rifles in the hands of Pinkertons with which to shoot down strikers in their own factories. I met men incoherent with indignation at the brutality of prize fighting, and who, at the same time, were parties to the adulteration of food that killed each year more babies than even red-handed Herod had killed.

I talked in hotels and clubs and homes and Pullmans and steamer chairs with captains of industry, and marveled at how little traveled they were in the realm of intellect. On the other

143   *What Life Means to Me*

hand, I discovered that their intellect, in the business sense, was abnormally developed. Also, I discovered that their morality, where business was concerned, was nil.

This delicate, aristocratic-featured gentleman, was a dummy director and a tool of corporations that secretly robbed widows and orphans. This gentleman, who collected fine editions and was an especial patron of literature, paid blackmail to a heavy-jowled, black-browed boss of a municipal machine. This editor, who published patent-medicine advertisements and did not dare print the truth in his paper about said patent medicines for fear of losing the advertising, called me a scoundrelly demagogue because I told him that his political economy was antiquated and that his biology was contemporaneous with Pliny.

This senator was the tool and the slave, the little puppet of a gross, uneducated machine boss; so was this governor and this supreme-court judge; and all three rode on railroad passes. This man, talking soberly and earnestly about the beauties of idealism and the goodness of God, had just betrayed his comrades in a business deal. This man, a pillar of the church and heavy contributor to foreign missions, worked his shop girls ten hours a day on a starvation wage and thereby directly encouraged prostitution. This man, who endowed chairs in universities, perjured himself in courts of law over a matter of dollars and cents. And this railroad magnate broke his word as a gentleman and a Christian when he granted a secret rebate to one of two captains of industry locked together in a struggle to the death.

It was the same everywhere, crime and betrayal, betrayal and crime — men who were alive, but who were neither clean nor noble, men who were clean and noble but who were not alive. Then there was a great, hopeless mass, neither noble nor alive, but merely clean. It did not sin positively nor deliberately; but it did sin passively and ignorantly by acquiescing in the current immorality and profiting thereby. Had it been noble and alive it would not have been ignorant, and it would have refused to share in the profits of betrayal and crime.

I discovered that I did not like to live on the parlor floor of society. Intellectually I was bored. Morally and spiritually I was sickened. I remembered my intellectuals and idealists, my unfrocked preachers, broken professors, and clean-minded, class-conscious workingmen. I remembered my days and nights of sunshine and starshine, where life was all a wild sweet wonder, a spiritual paradise of unselfish adventure and ethical romance. And I saw before me, ever blazing and burning, the Holy Grail.

So I went back to the working class, in which I had been born and where I belonged. I care no longer to climb. The imposing edifice of society above my head holds no delights for me. It is the foundation of the edifice that interests me. There I am content to labor, crowbar in hand, shoulder to shoulder with intellectuals, idealists, and class-conscious workingmen, getting a solid pry now and again and setting the whole edifice rocking. Some day, when we get a few more hands and crowbars to work, we'll topple it over, along with all its rotten life and unburied dead, its monstrous selfishness and sodden materialism. Then we'll cleanse the cellar and build a new habitation for mankind, in which there will be no parlor floor, in which all the rooms will be bright and airy, and where the air that is breathed will be clean, noble and alive.

Such is my outlook. I look forward to a time when man shall progress upon something worthier and higher than his stomach, when there will be a finer incentive to impel men to action than the incentive of to-day which is the incentive of the stomach. I retain my belief in the nobility and excellence of the human. I believe that spiritual sweetness and unselfishness will conquer the gross gluttony of to-day. And last of all, my faith is in the working class. As some Frenchman has said, "The stairway of time is ever echoing with the wooden shoe going up, the polished boot descending."

"The Apostate"

London wrote this story in late February or early March of 1906. Titled "The Rebel" in its early stages, the story became "The Apostate" before it was sent off to Woman's Home Companion *in the first week of April. The magazine accepted the story on April 22 and on May 1 paid London ten cents a word for the tale ($767.30). A year later he sold the story in England to* Lady's Realm *for 15/15/00. Unlike most of London's writings about tramps, "The Apostate" sold to the first magazine to which it was submitted. "No. 3. Magazine Sales. Feb. 1903 to July 1907," Box 102, and* Charmian London Diary, *March 23, 29, 1906, JLP, HEH.*

"Now I wake me up to work:
I pray the Lord I may not shirk.
If I should die before the night,
I pray the Lord my work's all right.
Amen."

"If you don't git up, Johnny, I won't give you a bite to eat."

The threat had no effect on the boy. He clung stubbornly to sleep, fighting for its oblivion as the dreamer fights for his dream. The boy's hands loosely clenched themselves, and he made feeble, spasmodic blows at the air. These blows were intended for his mother, but she betrayed practiced familiarity in avoiding them as she shook him roughly by the shoulder.

"Lemme 'lone!"

It was a cry that began, muffled, in the deeps of sleep; that swiftly rushed upward, like a wail, into passionate belligerence, and that died away and sank down into an inarticulate whine.

Source: *Woman's Home Companion*, XXXIII (September 1906), 5-7, 49.

It was a bestial cry, as of a soul in torment, filled with infinite protest and pain.

But she did not mind. She was a sad-eyed, tired-faced woman, and she had grown used to this task, which she repeated every day of her life. She got a grip on the bedclothes and tried to strip them down; but the boy, ceasing his punching, clung to them desperately. In a huddle at the foot of the bed, he still remained covered. Then she tried dragging the bedding to the floor. The boy opposed her. She braced herself. Hers was the superior weight, and the boy and bedding, the former instinctively followed the latter in order to shelter against the chill of the room that bit into his body.

As he toppled on the edge of the bed it seemed that he must fall head-first to the floor. But consciousness fluttered up in him. He righted himself and for a moment perilously balanced. Then he struck the floor on his feet. On the instant his mother seized him by the shoulders and shook him. Again his fists struck out, this time with more force and directness. At the same time his eyes opened. She released him. He was awake.

"All right," he mumbled.

She caught up the lamp and hurried out, leaving him in darkness.

"You'll be docked," she warned back to him.

He did not mind the darkness. When he had got into his clothes he went out into the kitchen. His tread was very heavy for so thin and light a boy. His legs dragged with their own weight, which seemed unreasonable because they were such skinny legs. He drew a broken-bottomed chair to the table.

"Johnny!" his mother called sharply.

He arose as sharply from the chair, and without a word went to the sink. It was a greasy, filthy sink. A smell came up from the outlet. He took no notice of it. That a sink should smell was to him part of the natural order, just as it was part of the natural order that the soap should be grimy with dish-water and hard to lather. Nor did he try very hard to make it lather. Several splashes of the cold water from the running faucet completed the function.

He did not wash his teeth. For that matter he had never seen a tooth-brush, nor did he know that there existed beings in the world who were guilty of so great a foolishness as tooth-washing.

"You might wash yourself wunst a day without bein' told," his mother complained.

She was holding a broken lid on the pot as she poured two cups of coffee. He made no remark, for this was a standing quarrel between them, and the one thing upon which his mother was hard as adamant. "Wunst" a day it was compulsory that he should wash his face. He dried himself on a greasy towel, damp and dirty and ragged, that left his face covered with shreds of lint.

"I wish we didn't live so far away," she said, as he sat down. "I try to do the best I can. You know that. But a dollar on the rent is such a savin', an' we've more room here. You know that."

He scarcely followed her. He had heard it all before, many times. The range of her thought was limited, and she was ever harking back to the hardship worked upon them by living so far from the mills.

"A dollar means more grub," he remarked sententiously. "I'd sooner do the walkin' an' git the grub."

He ate hurriedly, half-chewing the bread and washing the unmasticated chunks down with coffee. The hot and muddy liquid went by the name of coffee. Johnny thought it was coffee — and excellent coffee. That was one of the few of life's illusions that remained to him. He had never drunk real coffee in his life.

In addition to the bread there was a small piece of cold pork. His mother refilled his cup with coffee. As he was finishing the bread, he began to watch if more was forthcoming. She intercepted his questing glance.

"Now don't be hoggish, Johnny," was her comment. "You've had your share. Your brothers an' sisters are smaller'n you."

He did not answer the rebuke. He was not much of a talker. Also, he ceased his hungry glancing for more. He was uncomplaining, with a patience that was as terrible as the school in which it had been learned. He finished his coffee, wiped his mouth on the back of his hand, and started to arise.

"Wait a second," she said hastily. "I guess the loaf kin stand you another slice — a thin un."

There was legerdemain in her actions. With all the seeming of cutting a slice from the loaf for him, she put loaf and slice back in the bread-box and conveyed to him one of her own two slices. She believed she had deceived him, but he had noted her sleight-of-hand. Nevertheless he took the bread shamelessly. He had a philosophy that his mother, what of her chronic sickliness, was not much of an eater anyway.

She saw that he was chewing the bread dry, and reached over and emptied her coffee cup into his.

"Don't set good somehow on my stomach this mornin'," she explained.

A distant whistle, prolonged and shrieking, brought both of them to their feet. She glanced at the tin alarm-clock on the shelf. The hands stood at half-past five. The rest of the factory world was just arousing from sleep. She drew a shawl about her shoulders, and on her head put a dingy hat, shapeless and ancient.

"We've got to run," she said, turning the wick of the lamp and blowing down the chimney.

They groped their way out and down the stairs. It was clear and cold, and Johnny shivered at the first contact with the outside air. The stars had not yet begun to pale in the sky, and the city lay in blackness. Both Johnny and his mother shuffled their feet as they walked. There was no ambition in the leg muscles to swing the feet clear of the ground.

After fifteen silent minutes, his mother turned off to the right.

"Don't be late," was her final warning from out of the dark that was swallowing her up.

He made no response, steadily keeping on his way. In the factory quarter, doors were opening everywhere, and he was soon one of a multitude that pressed onward through the dark. As he entered the factory gate the whistle blew again. He glanced at the east. Across a ragged sky-line of housetops a pale light was beginning to creep. This much he saw of the day as he turned his back upon it and joined his work-gang.

He took his place in one of many long rows of machines. Before him, above a bin filled with small bobbins, were large bobbins, revolving rapidly. Upon these he wound the jute-twine of the small bobbins. The work was simple. All that was required was celerity. The small bobbins were emptied so rapidly, and there were so many large bobbins that did the emptying, that there were no idle moments.

He worked mechanically. When a small bobbin ran out, he used his left hand for a brake, stopping the large bobbin and at the same time, with thumb and forefinger, catching the flying end of twine. Also, at the same time, with his right hand, he caught up the loose twine-end on a small bobbin. These various acts with both hands were performed simultaneously and swiftly. Then there would come a flash of his hands as he looped the weaver's knot and released the bobbin. There was nothing difficult about weaver's knots. He once boasted he could tie them in his sleep. And for that matter, he sometimes did, toiling centuries long in a single night at tying an endless succession of weaver's knots.

Some of the boys shirked, wasting time and machinery by not replacing the small bobbins when they ran out. And there was an overseer to prevent this. He caught Johnny's neighbor at the trick and boxed his ears.

"Look at Johnny there — why ain't you like him?" the overseer wrathfully demanded.

Johnny's bobbins were running full blast, but he did not thrill at the indirect praise. There had been a time . . . but that was long ago, very long ago. His apathetic face was expressionless as he listened to himself being held up as a shining example. He was the perfect worker. He knew that. He had been told so, often. It was a commonplace, and besides it didn't seem to mean anything to him any more. From the perfect worker he had evolved into the perfect machine. When his work went wrong, it was with him as with the machine, due to faulty material. It would have been as possible for a perfect nail-die to cut imperfect nails as for him to make a mistake.

And small wonder. There had never been a time when he

had not been in intimate relationship with machines. Machinery had almost been bred into him, and at any rate he had been brought up on it. Twelve years before, there had been a small flutter of excitement in the loom-room of this very mill. Johnny's mother had fainted. They stretched her out on the floor in the midst of the shrieking machines. A couple of eldery women were called from their looms. The foreman assisted. And in a few minutes there was one more soul in the loom-room than had entered by the doors. It was Johnny, born with the pounding, crashing roar of the looms in his ears, drawing with his first breath the warm moist air that was thick with flying lint. He had coughed that first day in order to rid his lungs of the lint; and for the same reason he had coughed ever since.

The boy alongside of Johnny whimpered and sniffed. The boy's face was convulsed with hatred for the overseer who kept a threatening eye on him from a distance; but every bobbin was running full. The boy yelled terrible oaths into the whirling bobbins before him; but the sound did not carry half a dozen feet, the roaring of the room holding it in and containing it like a wall.

Of all this Johnny took no notice. He had a way of accepting things. Besides, things grow monotonous by repetition, and this particular happening he had witnessed many times. It seemed to him as useless to oppose the overseer as to defy the will of a machine. Machines were made to go in certain ways and to perform certain tasks. It was the same with the overseer.

But at eleven o'clock there was excitement in the room. In an apparently occult way the excitement instantly permeated everywhere. The one-legged boy who worked on the other side of Johnny bobbled swiftly across the floor to a bin-truck that stood empty. Into this he dived out of sight, crutch and all. The superintendent of the mill was coming along, accompanied by a young man. He was well-dressed and wore a starched shirt — a gentleman, in Johnny's classification of men, and also, "the Inspector."

He looked sharply at the boys as he passed along. Sometimes he stopped and asked questions. When he did so he was compelled to shout at the top of his lungs, at which moments his face was ludicrously contorted with the strain of making himself heard. His quick eye noted the empty machine alongside of Johnny's, but he said nothing. Johnny also caught his eye, and he stopped abruptly. He caught Johnny by the arm to draw him back a step from the machine; but with an exclamation of surprise he released the arm.

"Pretty skinny," the superintendent laughed anxiously.

"Pipe-stems," was the answer. "Look at those legs. The boy's got the rickets—incipient, but he's got them. If epilepsy doesn't get him in the end, it will be because tuberculosis gets him first."

Johnny listened, but did not understand. Furthermore he was not interested in future ills. There was an immediate and more serious ill that threatened him in the form of the inspector.

"Now, my boy, I want you to tell me the truth," the inspector said, or shouted, bending close to the boy's ear to make him hear. "How old are you?"

"Fourteen," Johnny lied, and he lied with the full force of his lungs. So loudly did he lie that it started him off in a dry, hacking cough that lifted the lint which had been settling in his lungs all morning.

"Looks sixteen at least," said the superintendent.

"Or sixty," snapped the inspector.

"He's always looked that way."

"How long?" asked the inspector quickly.

"For years. Never gets a bit older."

"Or younger, I daresay. I suppose he's worked here all those years?"

"Off and on—but that was before the new law was passed," the superintendent hastened to add.

"Machine idle?" the inspector asked, pointing at the unoccupied machine beside Johnny's, in which the part-filled bobbins were flying like mad.

"Looks that way." The superintendent motioned the overseer to him and shouted in his ear and pointed at the machine. "Machine's idle," he reported back to the inspector.

They passed on, and Johnny returned to his work, relieved in that the ill had been averted. But the one-legged boy was not so fortunate. The sharp-eyed inspector haled him out at arm's length from the bin-truck. His lips were quivering, and his face had all the expression of one upon whom was fallen profound and irremediable disaster. The overseer looked astounded, as though for the first time he had laid eyes on the boy, while the superintendent's face expressed shock and displeasure.

"I know him," the inspector said. "He's twelve years old. I've had him discharged from three factories inside the year. This makes the fourth."

He turned to the one-legged boy. "You promised me, word and honor, that you'd go to school."

The one-legged boy burst into tears. "Please, Mr. Inspector, two babies died on us, and we're awful poor."

"What makes you cough that way?" the inspector demanded, as though charging him with crime.

And as in denial of guilt, the one-legged boy replied, "It ain't nothin'. I jes' caught a cold last week, Mr. Inspector, that's all."

In the end the one-legged boy went out of the room with the inspector, the latter accompanied by the anxious and protesting superintendent. After that monotony settled down again. The long morning and the longer afternoon wore away and the whistle blew for quitting-time. Darkness had already fallen when Johnny passed out through the factory gate. In the interval the sun had made a golden ladder of the sky, flooded the world with its gracious warmth, and dropped down and disappeared in the west behind a ragged sky-line of housetops.

Supper was the family meal of the day — the one meal at which Johnny encountered his younger brothers and sisters. It partook of the nature of an encounter, to him, for he was very old, while they were distressingly young. He had no patience with their excessive and amazing juvenility. He did not understand it. His own childhood was too far behind him. He was like an old and irritable man, annoyed by the turbulence of their young spirits that was to him arrant silliness. He glowered silently over his food, finding compensation in the thought that they would soon have to go to work. That would take the edge off them and make them sedate and dignified — like him. Thus it was, after the fashion of the human, that Johnny made of himself a yardstick with which to measure the universe.

During the meal, his mother explained in various ways and with infinite repetition that she was trying to do the best she could; so that it was with relief, the scant meal ended, that Johnny shoved back his chair and arose. He debated for a moment between bed and the front door, and finally went out the latter. He did not go far. He sat down on the stoop, his knees drawn up and his narrow shoulders drooping forward, his elbows on his knees and the palms of his hands supporting his chin.

As he sat there he did no thinking. He was just resting. So far as his mind was concerned it was asleep. His brothers and sisters came out, and with other children played noisily about him. An electric globe on the corner lighted their frolics. He was peevish and irritable, that they knew; but the spirit of adventure lured them into teasing him. They joined hands before him, and, keeping time with their bodies, chanted in his face weird and uncomplimentary doggerel. At first he snarled curses at them — curses he had learned from the lips of various foremen. Finding this futile, and remembering his dignity, he relapsed into dogged silence.

His brother Will, next to him in age, having just passed his tenth birthday, was the ringleader. Johnny did not possess particularly kindly feelings toward him. His life had early been embittered by continual giving over and giving way to Will. He had a definite feeling that Will was greatly in his debt and was ungrateful about it. In his own playtime, far back in the dim past, he had been robbed of a large part of that playtime by being compelled to take care of Will. Will was a baby then, and then as now their mother had spent her days in the mills. To Johnny had fallen the part of little father and little mother as well.

Will seemed to show the benefit of the giving over and the giving way. He was well-built, fairly rugged, as tall as his elder brother and even heavier. It was as though the life-blood of the one had been diverted into the other's veins. And in spirits it was the same. Johnny was jaded, worn out, without resilience, while his younger brother seemed bursting and spilling over with exuberance.

The mocking chant rose louder and louder. Will leaned closer as he danced, thrusting out his tongue. Johnny's left arm shot out and caught the other around the neck. At the same time he rapped his bony fist to the other's nose. It was a pathetically bony fist, but that it was sharp to hurt was evidenced by the squeal of pain it produced. The other children were uttering frightened cries, while Johnny's sister, Jennie, had dashed into the house.

He thrust Will from him, kicked him savagely on the shins, then reached for him and slammed him face downward in the dirt. Nor did he release him till the face had been rubbed into the dirt several times. Then the mother arrived, an anemic whirlwind of solicitude and maternal wrath.

"Why can't he leave me alone?" was Johnny's reply to her upbraiding. "Can't he see I'm tired?"

"I'm as big as you," Will raged in her arms, his face a mess of tears, dirt and blood. "I'm as big as you now, an' I'm goin' to git bigger. Then I'll lick you — see if I don't."

"You ought to be to work, seein' how big you are," Johnny snarled. "That's what's the matter with you. You ought to be to work. An' it's up to your ma to put you to work."

"But he's too young," she protested. "He's only a little boy."

"I was younger'n him when I started to work."

Johnny's mouth was open, further to express the sense of unfairness that he felt, but the mouth closed with a snap. He turned gloomily on his heel and stalked into the house and to bed. The door of his room was open to let in warmth from the kitchen. As he undressed in the semi-darkness he could hear his mother talking with a neighbor woman who had dropped in. His mother was crying, and her speech was punctuated with spiritless sniffles.

"I can't make out what's gittin' into Johnny," he could hear her say. "He didn't used to be this way. He was a patient little angel.

"An' he *is* a good boy," she hastened to defend. "He's worked faithful, an' he did go to work too young. But it wasn't my fault. I do the best I can, I'm sure."

Prolonged sniffling from the kitchen, and Johnny murmured to himself as his eyelids closed down, "You betcher life I've worked faithful."

The next morning he was torn bodily by his mother from the grip of sleep. Then came the meager breakfast, the tramp through the dark, and the pale glimpse of day across the house-tops as he turned his back on it and went in through the factory gate. It was another day, of all the days, and all the days were alike.

And yet there had been variety in his life — at the times he changed from one job to another, or was taken sick. When he was six he was little mother and father to Will and the other children still younger. At seven he went into the mills — winding bobbins. When he was eight he got work in another mill. His new job was marvelously easy. All he had to do was to sit down with a little stick in his hand and guide a stream of cloth that flowed past him. This stream of cloth came out of the maw of a machine, passed over a hot roller, and went on its way elsewhere. But he sat always in the one place, beyond the reach of daylight, a gas-jet flaring over him, himself part of the mechanism.

He was very happy at that job, in spite of the moist heat, for he was still young and in possession of dreams and illusions. And wonderful dreams he dreamed as he watched the steaming cloth streaming endlessly by. But there was no exercise about the work, no call upon his mind, and he dreamed less and less, while his mind grew torpid and drowsy. Nevertheless, he earned two dollars a week, and two dollars represented the difference between acute starvation and chronic underfeeding.

But when he was nine, he lost his job. Measles was the cause of it. After he recovered he got work in a glass factory. The pay was better, and the work demanded skill. It was piece-work, and the more skilful he was the bigger wages he earned.

Here was incentive. And under this incentive he developed into a remarkable worker.

It was simple work, the tying of glass stoppers into small bottles. At his waist he carried a bundle of twine. He held the bottles between his knees so that he might work with both hands. Thus, in a sitting position and bending over his own knees, his narrow shoulders grew humped and his chest was contracted for ten hours each day. This was not good for the lungs, but he tied three hundred dozen bottles a day.

The superintendent was very proud of him, and brought visitors to look at him. In ten hours three hundred dozen bottles passed through his hands. This meant that he had attained machine-like perfection. All waste movements were eliminated. Every motion of his thin arms, every movement of a muscle in the thin fingers, was swift and accurate. He worked at high tension, and the result was that he grew nervous. At night his muscles twitched in his sleep, and in the daytime he could not relax and rest. He remained keyed up and his muscles continued to twitch. Also he grew sallow and his lint-cough grew worse. Then pneumonia laid hold of his feeble lungs within the contracted chest, and he lost his job in the glass-works.

Now he had returned to the jute-mills, where he had first begun with winding bobbins. But promotion was waiting for him. He was a good worker. He would next go on the starcher, and later he would go into the loom-room. There was nothing after that except increased efficiency.

The machinery ran faster than when he had first gone to work, and his mind ran slower. He no longer dreamed at all, though his earlier years had been full of dreaming. Once he had been in love. It was when he first began guiding the cloth over the hot roller, and it was with the daughter of the superintendent. She was much older than he, a young woman, and he had seen her at a distance only a paltry half dozen times. But that made no difference. On the surface of the cloth stream that poured past him, he pictured radiant futures wherein he performed prodigies of toil, invented miraculous machines, won to the mastership of the mills, and in the end took her in his arms and kissed her soberly on the brow.

But that was all in the long ago, before he had grown too old and tired to love. Also, she had married and gone away, and his mind had gone to sleep. Yet it had been a wonderful experience, and he used often to look back upon it as other men and women look back upon the time they believed in fairies. He had never believed in fairies nor Santa Claus; but he had believed implicitly in the smiling futures his imagination had wrought into the steaming cloth stream.

He had become a man very early in life. At seven, when he drew his first wages, began his adolescence. A certain feeling of independence crept up in him, and the relationship between him and his mother changed. Somehow, as an earner and bread-winner, doing his own work in the world, he was more like an equal with her. Manhood, full-blown manhood, had come when he was eleven, at which time he had gone to work on the night-shift for six months. No child works on the night-shift and remains a child.

There had been several great events in his life. One of these had been when his mother bought some California prunes. Two others had been the two times when she cooked custard. Those had been events. He remembered them kindly. And at that time his mother had told him of a blissful dish she would sometime make — "floating island," she had called it, "better than custard." For years he had looked forward to the day when he would sit down to the table with floating island before him, until at last he had relegated the idea of it to the limbo of unattainable ideals.

Once he found a silver quarter lying on the sidewalk. That, also, was a great event in his life, withal a tragic one. He knew his duty on the instant the silver flashed on his eyes, before even he had picked it up. At home, as usual, there was not enough to eat, and home he should have taken it as he did his wages every Saturday night. Right conduct in this case was obvious; but he never had any spending of his money, and he was suffering from candy-hunger. He was ravenous for the sweets that only on red-letter days he had ever tasted in his life.

He did not attempt to deceive himself. He knew it was sin, and deliberately he sinned when he went on a fifteen-cent candy debauch. Ten cents he saved for a future debauch; but not being accustomed to the carrying of money, he lost the ten cents. This occurred at the time when he was suffering all the torments of conscience, and it was to him an act of divine retribution. He had a frightened sense of the closeness of an awful and wrathful God. God had seen, and God had been swift to punish, denying him even the full wages of sin.

In memory he always looked back upon that event as the one great criminal deed of his life, and at the recollection his conscience always awoke and gave him another twinge. It was the one skeleton in his closet. Also, being so made and circumstanced, he looked back upon the deed with regret. He was dissatisfied with the manner in which he had spent the quarter. He could have invested it better, and, out of his later knowledge of the quickness of God, he would have beaten God out by spending the whole quarter at one fell swoop. In retrospect he spent the quarter a thousand times and each time to better advantage.

There was one other memory of the past, dim and faded, but stamped into his soul everlastingly by the savage feet of his father. It was more like a nightmare than a remembered vision of a concrete thing — more like the race-memory of man that makes him fall in his sleep and that goes back to his arboreal ancestry.

This particular memory never came to Johnny in broad daylight when he was wide awake. It came at night, in bed, at the moment that his consciousness was sinking down and losing itself in sleep. It always aroused him to frightened wakefulness, and for the moment, in the first sickening start, it seemed to him that he lay crosswise on the foot of the bed. In the bed were the vague forms of his father and mother. He never saw what his father looked like. He had but one impression of his father, and that was that he had savage and pitiless feet.

His earlier memories lingered with him, but he had no late memories. All days were alike. Yesterday or last year were the same as a thousand years — or a minute. Nothing ever happened. There were no events to mark the march of time. Time did not march. It stood always still. It was only the whirling machines that moved, and they moved nowhere — in spite of the fact that they moved faster.

When he was fourteen he went to work on the starcher. It was a colossal event. Something had at last happened that could be remembered beyond a night's sleep or a week's pay-day. It marked an era. It was a machine Olympiad, a thing to date from. "When I went to work on the starcher," or, "after," or "before I went to work on the starcher," were sentences often on his lips.

He celebrated his sixteenth birthday by going into the loom-room and taking a loom. Here was an incentive again, for it was piece-work. And he excelled, because the clay of him had been molded by the mills into the perfect machine. At the end of three months he was running two looms, and, later, three and four.

At the end of his second year at the looms, he was turning out more yards than any other weaver, and more than twice as much as some of the less skillful ones. And at home things began to prosper as he approached the full stature of his earning power. Not, however, that his increased earnings were in excess of need. The children were growing up. They ate more. And they were going to school, and school-books cost money. And somehow, the faster he worked, the faster climbed the prices of things. Even the rent went up, though the house had fallen from bad to worse disrepair.

He had grown taller; but with his increased height he seemed leaner than ever. Also, he was more nervous. With the nervousness increased his peevishness and irritability. The children had learned by many bitter lessons to fight shy of him. His mother respected him for his earning power, but somehow her respect was tinctured with fear.

161   *The Apostate*

There was no joyousness in life for him. The procession of the days he never saw. The nights he slept away in twitching unconsciousness. The rest of the time he worked, and his consciousness was machine consciousness. Outside this his mind was a blank. He had no ideals, and but one illusion, namely, that he drank excellent coffee. He was a work-beast. He had no mental life whatever; yet deep down in the crypts of his mind, unknown to him, were being weighed and sifted every hour of his toil, every movement of his hands, every twitch of his muscles, and preparations were making for a future course of action that would amaze him and all his little world.

It was in the late spring that he came home from work one night aware of an unusual tiredness. There was a keen expectancy in the air as he sat down to the table, but he did not notice. He went through the meal in moody silence, mechanically eating what was before him. The children um'd and ah'd and made smacking noises with their mouths. But he was deaf to them.

"D'ye know what you're eatin'?" his mother demanded at last, desperately.

He looked vacantly at the dish before him, and vacantly at her.

"Floatin' island," she announced triumphantly.

"Oh," he said.

"Floatin' island!" the children chorused loudly.

"Oh," he said. And after two or three mouthfuls, he added, "I guess I ain't hungry to-night."

He dropped the spoon, shoved back his chair, and arose wearily from the table.

"An' I guess I'll go to bed."

His feet dragged more heavily than usual as he crossed the kitchen floor. Undressing was a Titan's task, a monstrous futility, and he wept weakly as he crawled into bed, one shoe still on. He was aware of a rising, swelling something inside his head that made his brain thick and fuzzy. His lean fingers felt as big as his wrist, while in the ends of them was a remoteness of sensation vague and fuzzy like his brain. The small of his back ached intolerably. All his bones ached. He ached everywhere. And in his head began the shrieking, pounding, crashing, roaring of a million looms. All space was filled with flying shuttles. They darted in and out, intricately, amongst the stars. He worked a thousand looms himself, and ever they speeded up, faster and faster, and his brain unwound, faster and faster, and became the thread that fed the thousand flying shuttles.

He did not go to work next morning. He was too busy weaving colossally on the thousand looms that ran inside his head. His mother went to work, but first she sent for the doctor. It was a severe attack of la grippe, he said. Jennie served as nurse and carried out his instructions.

It was a very severe attack, and it was a week before Johnny dressed and tottered feebly across the floor. Another week, the doctor said, and he would be fit to return to work. The foreman of the loom-room visited him on Sunday afternoon, the first day of his convalescence. The best weaver in her room, the foreman told his mother. His job would be held for him. He could come back to work a week from Monday.

"Why don't you thank 'm, John?" his mother asked anxiously.

"He's ben that sick he ain't himself yet," she explained apologetically to the visitor.

Johnny sat hunched up and gazing steadfastly at the floor. He sat in the same position long after the foreman had gone. It was warm outdoors, and he sat on the stoop in the afternoon. Sometimes his lips moved. He seemed lost in endless calculations.

Next morning, after the day grew warm, he took his seat on the stoop. He had pencil and paper this time with which to continue his calculations, and he calculated painfully and amazingly.

"What comes after millions?" he asked at noon, when Will came home from school. "An' how d'ye work 'em?"

That afternoon finished his task. Each day, but without paper and pencil, he returned to the stoop. He was greatly absorbed in the one tree that grew across the street. He studied it for hours at a time, and was unusually interested when the wind swayed its branches and fluttered its leaves. Throughout the week he seemed lost in a great communion with himself. On Sunday, sitting on the stoop, he laughed aloud, several times, to the perturbation of his mother, who had not heard him laugh in years.

Next morning, in the early darkness, she came to his bed to rouse him. He had had his fill of sleep all week and awoke easily. He made no struggle, nor did he attempt to hold onto the bedding when she stripped it from him. He lay quietly, and spoke quietly.

"It ain't no use, ma."

"You'll be late," she said, under the impression that he was still stupid with sleep.

"I'm awake, ma, an' I tell you it ain't no use. You might as well lemme alone. I ain't goin' to git up."

But you'll lose your job!" she cried.

"I ain't goin' to git up," he repeated in a strange, passionless voice.

She did not go to work herself that morning. This was sickness beyond any sickness she had ever known. Fever and delirium she could understand; but this was insanity. She pulled the bedding up over him and sent Jennie for the doctor.

When that person arrived Johnny was sleeping gently, and gently he awoke and allowed his pulse to be taken.

"Nothing the matter with him," the doctor reported. "Badly debilitated, that's all. Not much meat on his bones."

"He's always been that way," his mother volunteered.

"Now go 'way, ma, an' let me finish my snooze."

Johnny spoke sweetly and placidly, and sweetly and placidly he rolled over on his side and went to sleep.

At ten o'clock he awoke and dressed himself. He walked out into the kitchen, where he found his mother with a frightened expression on her face.

"I'm goin' away, ma," he announced, "an' I jes' want to say good-by."

She threw her apron over her head and sat down suddenly and wept. He waited patiently.

"I might a-known it," she was sobbing.

"Where?" she finally asked, removing the apron from her

head and gazing up at him with a stricken face in which there was little curiosity.

"I don't know — anywhere."

As he spoke the tree across the street appeared with dazzling brightness on his inner vision. It seemed to lurk just under his eyelids, and he could see it whenever he wished.

"An' your job?" she quavered.

"I ain't never goin' to work again."

"My God, Johnny!" she wailed, "don't say that!"

What he had said was blasphemy to her. As a mother who hears her child deny God, was Johnny's mother shocked by his words.

"What's got into you, anyway?" she demanded, with a lame attempt at imperativeness.

"Figures," he answered. "Jes' figures. I've ben doin' a lot of figurin' this week, an' it's most surprisin'."

"I don't see what that's got to do with it," she sniffled.

Johnny smiled patiently, and his mother was aware of a distinct shock at the persistent absence of his peevishness and irritability.

"I'll show you," he said. "I'm plum tired out. What makes me tired? Moves. I've ben movin' ever since I was born. I'm tired of movin', an' I ain't goin' to move any more. Remember when I worked in the glasshouse? I used to do three hundred dozen a day. Now I reckon I made about ten different moves to each bottle. That's thirty-six thousan' moves a day. Ten days, three hundred an' sixty thousan' moves. One month, one million an' eighty thousan' moves. Chuck out the eighty thousan'—" he spoke with the complacent beneficence of a philanthropist — "chuck out the eighty thousan', that leaves a million moves a month — twelve million moves a year.

"At the looms I'm movin' twic'st as much. That makes twenty-five million moves a year, an' it seems to me I've ben a-movin' that way 'most a million years.

"Now this week I ain't moved at all. I ain't made one move in hours an' hours. I tell you it was swell, jes' settin' there, hours an' hours, an' doin' nothin'. I ain't never ben happy before. I never had any time. I've ben movin' all the time. That ain't no way to be happy. An' I ain't goin' to do it any more. I'm jes' goin' to set, an' set, an' rest, an' rest, an' then rest some more."

"But what's goin' to come of Will an' the childern?" she asked despairingly.

"That's it, 'Will an' the childern,' " he repeated.

But there was no bitterness in his voice. He had long known his mother's ambition for the younger boy, but the thought of it no longer rankled. Nothing mattered any more. Not even that.

"I know, ma, what you've ben plannin' for Will — keepin' him in school to make a bookkeeper out of him. But it ain't no use. I've quit. He's got to go to work."

"An' after I have brung you up the way I have," she wept, starting to cover her head with the apron and changing her mind.

"You never brung me up," he answered with sad kindliness. "I brung myself up, ma, an' I brung up Will. He's bigger'n me, an' heavier, an' taller. When I was a kid I reckon I didn't git enough to eat. When he come along an' was a kid, I was workin' an' earnin' grub for him, too. But that's done with. Will can go to work, same as me, or he can go to hell, I don't care which. I'm tired. I'm goin' now. Ain't you goin' to say good-by?"

She made no reply. The apron had gone over her head again and she was crying. He paused a moment in the doorway.

"I'm sure I done the best I knew how," she was sobbing.

He passed out of the house and down the street. A wan delight came into his face at the sight of the lone tree. "Jes' ain't goin' to do nothin'," he said to himself, half aloud, in a crooning tone. He glanced wistfully up at the sky, but the bright sun dazzled and blinded him.

It was a long walk he took, and he did not walk fast. It took him past the jute-mill. The muffled roar of the loom-room came to his ears, and he smiled. It was a gentle, placid smile. He hated no one, not even the pounding, shrieking machines. There was no bitterness in him, nothing but an inordinate hunger for rest.

The houses and factories thinned out and the open spaces

increased as he approached the country. At last the city was behind him, and he was walking down a leafy lane beside the railroad track. He did not walk like a man. He did not look like a man. He was a travesty of the human. It was a twisted and stunted and nameless piece of life that shambled like a sickly ape, arms loose-hanging, stoop-shouldered, narrow-chested, grotesque and terrible.

He passed by a small railroad station and lay down in the grass under a tree. All afternoon he lay there. Sometimes he dozed, with muscles that twitched in his sleep. When awake, he lay without movement, watching the birds or looking up at the sky through the branches of the tree above him. Once or twice he laughed aloud, but without relevance to anything he had seen or felt.

After twilight had gone, in the first darkness of the night, a freight train rumbled into the station. While the engine was switching cars onto the side-track, Johnny crept along the side of the train. He pulled open the side-door of an empty box-car and awkwardly and laboriously climbed in. He closed the door. The engine whistled. Johnny was lying down, and in the darkness he smiled.

"The Hobo and the Fairy"

In October of 1910 London tried to publish this story in Woman's Home Companion *(which had taken "The Apostate" in 1906), but when the magazine rejected the story he sent it to* Saturday Evening Post. *In December of 1910 the* Post *accepted the tale and paid London his usual ten cents per word ($507.70). One year later the story was sold in England to* Cassell's Magazine *for 15/15/00. No. 4. Magazine Sales, March 1908 to March 1916, Box 102, JLP, HEH.*

He lay on his back. So heavy was his sleep that the stamp of hoofs and cries of the drivers from the bridge that crossed the creek did not rouse him. Wagon after wagon loaded high with grapes, passed the bridge on the way up the valley to the winery, and the coming of each wagon was like an explosion of sound and commotion in the lazy quiet of the afternoon.

But the man was undisturbed. His head had slipped from the folded newspaper, and the straggling, unkempt hair was matted with the foxtails and the burs of the dry grass on which it lay. He was not a pretty sight. His mouth was open, disclosing a gap in the upper row where several teeth at some time had been knocked out. He breathed stertorously, at times grunting and moaning with the pain of his sleep. Also, he was very restless, tossing his arms about, making jerky, half-convulsive movements, and at times rolling his head from side to side in the burs. This restlessness seemed occasioned partly by some internal discomfort, and partly by the sun that streamed down on his face, and by the

Source: *Saturday Evening Post, CLXXXIII* (February 11, 1911), 12-13, 41-42.

flies that buzzed and lighted and crawled upon the nose and cheeks and eyelids. There was no other place for them to crawl, for the rest of the face was covered with matted beard, slightly grizzled, but greatly dirt-stained and weather discolored.

The cheekbones were blotched with the blood congested by the debauch that was evidently being slept off. This, too, accounted for the persistence with which the flies clustered around the mouth, lured by the alcohol-laden exhalations. He was a powerfully-built man, thick-necked, broad-shouldered, with sinewy wrists and toil-distorted hands. Yet the distortion was not due to recent toil, nor were the calluses other than ancient that showed under the dirt of the one palm upturned. From time to time this hand clinched tightly and spasmodically into a fist, large, heavy-boned and wicked-looking.

The man lay in the dry grass of a tiny glade that ran down to the tree-fringed bank of the stream. On each side of the glade was a fence, of the old stake-and-rider type, though little of it was to be seen, so thickly was it overgrown by wild blackberry bushes, scrubby oaks, and young madroña trees. In the rear a gate through a low paling-fence led to a snug, squat bungalow, built in the California Spanish style and seeming to have been compounded directly from the landscape of which it was so justly a part. Neat and trim and modestly sweet was the bungalow, redolent of comfort and repose, telling with quiet certitude of someone that knew and that had sought and found.

Through the gate and into the glade came as dainty a little maiden as ever stepped out of an illustration made especially to show how dainty little maidens may be. Eight years she might have been, and possibly a trifle more, or less. Her little waist and little black-stockinged calves showed how delicately fragile she was; but the fragility was of mould only. There was no hint of anaemia in the clear, healthy complexion or in the quick, tripping step. She was a little, delicious blonde, with hair spun of gossamer gold and wide blue eyes that were but slightly veiled by the long lashes. Her expression was of sweetness and happiness; it belonged by right to any face that was sheltered in the bungalow.

She carried a parasol, which she was careful not to tear against the scrubby branches and bramble-bushes as she sought for wild poppies along the edge of the fence. They were late poppies, a third generation, which had been unable to resist the call of the warm October sun.

Having gathered along one fence she turned to cross to the opposite fence. Midway in the glade she came upon the tramp. Her startle was merely a startle. There was no fear in it. She stood and looked long and curiously at the forbidding spectacle and was about to turn back when the sleeper moved restlessly and rolled his head among the burs. She noted the sun on his face and the buzzing flies; her face grew solicitous and for a moment she debated with herself. Then she tiptoed to his side, interposed the parasol between him and the sun and brushed away the flies. After a time, for greater ease, she sat down beside him.

An hour passed, during which she occasionally shifted the parasol from one tired hand to the other. At first the sleeper had been restless; but, shielded from the flies and sun, his breathing became gentler and his movements ceased. Several times, however, he really frightened her. The first was the worst, coming abruptly and without warning. "How deep! How deep!" the man murmured from some profound of dream. The parasol was agitated, but the little girl controlled herself and continued her self-appointed ministrations.

Another time it was a gritting of teeth, as of some intolerable agony. So terribly did the teeth crunch and grind together that it seemed they must crash into fragments. A little later he suddenly stiffened out. The hands clenched and the face set with the savage resolution of the dream. The eyelids, trembling from the shock of the fantasy, seemed about to open, but did not. Instead, the lips muttered:

"No! No! And once more no! I won't peach!" The lips paused, then went on. "You might as well tie me up, warden, and cut me to pieces. That's all you can get outa me — blood. That's all any of you-uns has ever got outa me in this hole."

After this outburst the man slept gently on while the little girl still held the parasol aloft and looked down with a great wonder at the frowsy, unkempt creature, trying to reconcile it with the little part of life that she knew. To her ears came the cries of men the stamp of hoofs on the bridge and the creak and groan of wagons heavy-laden. It was a breathless, California Indian-summer day. Light fleeces of cloud drifted in the azure sky, but to the west heavy cloudbanks threatened with rain. A bee droned lazily by. From farther thickets came the calls of quail and from the fields the songs of meadowlarks; and, oblivious to it all, slept Ross Shanklin — Ross Shanklin, the tramp and outcast, ex-convict 4379, the bitter and unbreakable one who had defied all keepers and survived all brutalities.

Texan-born, of the old pioneer stock that was always tough and stubborn, he had been unfortunate. At seventeen years of age he had been apprehended for horse-stealing. Also, he had been convicted of stealing seven horses that he had not stolen, and he had been sentenced to fourteen years' imprisonment. This was severe under any circumstance, but with him it had been especially severe because there had been no prior convictions against him. The sentiment of the people who believed him guilty had been that two years was adequate punishment for the youth, but the county attorney, paid according to the convictions he secured, had made seven charges against him and earned seven fees, which goes to show that the county attorney valued twelve years of Ross Shanklin's life at less than a few dollars.

Young Ross Shanklin had toiled in hell; he had escaped more than once and he had been caught and sent back to toil in other and various hells. He had been triced up and lashed till he fainted, had been revived and lashed again. He had been in the dungeon ninety days at a time. He had experienced the torment of the strait jacket. He knew what the humming bird was. He had been farmed out as a chattel by the state of the contractors. He had been trailed through swamps by bloodhounds. Twice he had been shot. For six years on end he had cut a cord and a half of wood each day in a convict lumber camp. Sick or well, he had cut that cord and a half, or paid for it under a whip-lash, knotted and pickled.

And Ross Shanklin had not sweetened under the treatment. He had sneered, and cursed and defied. He had seen convicts, after the guards had manhandled them, crippled in body for life or left to maunder in mind to the end of their days. He had seen convicts, even his own cellmate goaded to murder by their keepers, go to the gallows. He had been in a break in which eleven of his kind were shot down. He had been through a mutiny, where, in the prison yard, with gatling guns trained upon them, three hundred convicts had been disciplined with pickhandles wielded by brawny guards.

He had known every infamy of human cruelty and through it all he had never been broken. He had resented and fought to the last; until, embittered and bestial, the day came when he was discharged. Five dollars were given him in payment for the years of his labor and the flower of his manhood. And he had worked little in the years that followed. Work he despised. He tramped, begged and stole, lied or threatened, as the case might warrant; and drank to besottedness whenever he got the chance.

The little girl was looking at him when he awoke. Like a wild animal, all of him was awake the instant he opened his eyes. The first he saw was the parasol, strangely obtruded between him and the sky. He did not start or move, though his whole body seemed slightly to tense. His eyes followed down the parasol handle to the tight-clutched little fingers and along the arm to the child's face. Straight and unblinking, he looked into her eyes; and she, returning the look, was chilled and frightened by his glittering eyes, cold and harsh, withal bloodshot, and with no hint in them of the warm humanness she had been accustomed to see and feel in human eyes. They were the true prison eyes — the eyes of a man who had learned to talk little; who had forgotten almost how to talk.

"Hello!" he said finally, making no effort to change his position. "What game are you up to?" His voice was gruff, and at first it had been harsh; but it softened queerly in a feeble attempt at forgotten kindliness.

"How do you do?" she said. "I'm not playing. The sun was on your face, and mamma says one oughtn't to sleep in the sun."

The sweet clearness of her child's voice was pleasant to him and he wondered why he had never noticed it in children's voices before. He sat up slowly and stared at her. He felt that he ought to say something, but speech with him was a reluctant thing.

"I hope you slept well," she said gravely.

"I sure did," he answered, never taking his eyes from her, amazed at the fairness and delicacy of her. "How long was you holdin' that contraption up over me?"

"O-oh," she debated with herself, "a long, long time! I thought you would never wake up."

"And I thought you was a fairy when I first seen you."

He felt elated at his contribution to the conversation.

"No, not a fairy," she smiled.

He was thrilled in a strange numb way at the immaculate whiteness of her small, even teeth.

"I was just the good Samaritan," she added.

"I reckon I never heard of that party."

He was cudgeling his brains to keep the conversation going. Never having been at close quarters with a child since he was man-grown, he found it difficult.

"What a funny man not to know about the good Samaritan! Don't you remember? A certain man went down to Jericho —"

"I reckon I've been there," he interrupted.

"I knew you were a traveler," she cried, clapping her hands. "Maybe you saw the exact spot."

"What spot?"

"Why, where he fell among thieves and was left half dead. And then the good Samaritan went to him and bound up his wounds, and poured in oil and wine — was that olive oil, do you think?"

He shook his head slowly.

"I reckon you got me there. Olive oil is something the dagos cooks with. I never heard it was good for busted heads."

She considered his statement for a moment. "Well," she announced, "we use olive oil in our cooking; so we must be dagos. I never knew what they were before. I thought it was slang."

"And the Samaritan dumped oil on his head?" the tramp muttered reminiscently. "Seems to me I recollect a sky pilot sayin' something about that old gent. D'ye know, I've been looking for him off'n' on all my life and never scared up hide or hair of him. They ain't no more Samaritans."

"Wasn't I one?" she asked quickly.

He looked at her steadily, with a great curiosity and wonder. Her ear, by a movement exposed to the sun, was transparent. It seemed he could almost see through it. He was amazed at the delicacy of her coloring, at the blue of her eyes, at the dazzle of the sun-touched golden hair; and he was astounded by her fragility. It came to him that she was easily broken. His eye went quickly from his huge, gnarled paw to her tiny hand, in which it seemed to him he could almost see the blood circulate. He knew the power in his muscles and he knew the tricks and turns by which men use their bodies to ill-treat men; in fact, he knew little else and his mind for the time ran in its customary channel. It was his way of measuring the beautiful strangeness of her. He calculated a grip — and not a strong one — that could grind her little fingers to pulp. He thought of fist-blows he had given to men's heads and received on his own head, and felt that the least of them could shatter hers like an eggshell. He scanned her little shoulders and slim waist, and knew in all certitude that with his two hands he could rend her to pieces.

"Wasn't I one?" she insisted again.

He came back to himself with a shock — or away from himself as the case happened. He was loath that the conversation should cease.

"What?" he answered. "Oh, yes; you bet you was a Samaritan, if you didn't have no olive oil." He remembered what his mind had been dwelling on, and asked: "But ain't you afraid?"

She looked at him as if she did not understand.

"Of — of me?" he added lamely.

She laughed merrily.

"Mamma says never to be afraid of anything. She says that if you're good — and you think good of other people — they'll be good too."

"And you was thinkin' good of me when you kept the sun off," he marvelled.

"But it's hard to think good of bees and nasty crawly things," she confessed.

"But there's men that is nasty and crawly things," he argued.

"Mamma says no. She says there's good in every one."

"I bet you she locks the house up tight at night just the same," he proclaimed triumphantly.

"But she doesn't. Mamma isn't afraid of anything. That's why she lets me play out here alone when I want. Why, we had a robber once. Mamma got right up and found him. And what do you think? He was only a poor hungry man. And she got him plenty to eat from the pantry; and afterwards she got him work to do."

Ross Shanklin was stunned. The vista shown him of human nature was unthinkable. It had been his lot to live in a world of suspicion and hatred, of evil-believing and evil-doing. It had been his experience, slouching along village streets at nightfall, to see little children, screaming with fear, run from him to their mothers. He had even seen grown women shrink aside from him as he passed along the sidewalk.

He was aroused by the girl clapping her hands, as she cried out:

"I know what you are! You're an open-air crank! That's why you were sleeping here in the grass."

He felt a grim desire to laugh, but repressed it.

"And that's what tramps are — open-air cranks," she continued. "I often wondered. Mamma believes in the open air. I sleep on the porch at night. So does she. This is our land. You must have climbed the fence. Mamma lets me when I put on my climbers — they're bloomers, you know. But you ought to be told something. A person doesn't know when they snore because they're asleep. But you do worse than that. You grit your teeth. That's bad. Whenever you are going to sleep you must think to yourself, 'I won't grit my teeth; I won't grit my teeth,' over and over, just like that; and by–and–by you'll get out of the habit."

"All bad things are habits. And so are all good things. And it depends on us what kind our habits are going to be. I used to pucker my eyebrows — wrinkle them all up; but mamma said I must overcome that habit. She said that when my eyebrows were wrinkled it was an advertisement that my brain was wrinkled inside and that it wasn't good to have wrinkles in the brain. Then she smoothed my eyebrows with her hand and said I must always think smooth — smooth inside and smooth outside. And, do you know, it was easy. I haven't wrinkled my brows for ever so long. I've heard about filling teeth by thinking, but I don't believe that. Neither does mamma.

She paused, rather out of breath. Nor did he speak. Her flow of talk had been too much for him. Also, sleeping drunkenly, with open mouth had made him very thirsty; but, rather than lose one precious moment, he endured the torment of his scorching throat. He licked his dry lips and struggled for speech.

"What is your name?" he managed at last.

"Joan."

She looked her own question at him and it was not necessary to voice it.

"Mine is Ross Shanklin," he volunteered, for the first time in forgotten years giving his real name.

"I suppose you've traveled a lot."

"To be sure I have, but not as much as I might have wanted to."

"Papa always wanted to travel, but he was too busy at the office. He never could get much time. He went to Europe once with mamma. That was before I was born. It takes money to travel."

Ross Shanklin did not know whether to agree with this statement or not.

"But it doesn't cost tramps much for expenses." She took the thought away from him. "Is that why you tramp?"

He nodded and licked his lips.

"Mamma says it's too bad that men must tramp to look for work; but there's lots of work now in the country. All the farmers in the valley are trying to get men. Have you been working?"

He shook his head, angry with himself that he should feel shame at the confession when his savage reasoning told him he was right in despising work. But this was followed by another thought. This beautiful little creature was some man's child. She was one of the rewards of work.

"I wish I had a little girl like you," he blurted out, stirred by a sudden consciousness of his newborn passion for paternity. "I'd work my hands off. I— I'd do anything!"

She considered his case with fitting gravity.

"Then you aren't married?"

"Nobody would have me."

"Yes they would — if — —"

She did not turn up her nose, but she favored his dirt and rags with a look of disapprobation he could not mistake.

"Go on," he half shouted, "shoot it into me! If I was washed — — if I wore good clothes — if I was respectable — if I had a job and worked regular — if I wasn't what I am!"

To each statement she nodded.

"Well, I ain't that kind," he rushed on. "I'm no good. I'm a tramp. I don't want to work — that's what — and I like dirt." Her face was eloquent with reproach as she said:

"Then you were only making believe when you wished you had a little girl like me?"

This left him speechless, for he knew, in all the deeps of his newfound passion, that was just what he did want.

With ready tact, noting his discomfort, she sought to change the subject.

"What do you think of God?" she asked.

"I ain't never met Him. What do you think about him?"

His reply was evidently angry and she was frank in her disapproval.

"You are very strange," she said. "You get angry so easily. I never saw anybody before that got angry about God, or work, or being clean."

"He never done anything for me," he muttered resentfully. He cast back in quick review of the long years of toil in the convict camps and mines. "And work never done anything for me neither."

An embarrassing silence fell.

He looked at her, numb and hungry with the stir of the father-love, sorry for his ill temper, puzzling his brain for something to say. She was looking off and away at the clouds and he devoured her with his eyes. He reached out stealthily and rested one grimy hand on the very edge of her little dress.

It seemed to him that she was the most wonderful thing in the world. The quail still called from the coverts, and the harvest sounds seemed abrupty to become very loud. A great loneliness oppressed him.

"I'm — I'm no good!" he murmured, huskily and repentantly.

But, beyond a glance from her blue eyes, she took no notice. The silence was more embarrassing than ever. He felt that he could give the world just to touch with his lips that hem of her dress where his hand rested, but he was afraid of frightening her. He fought to find something to say, licking his parched lips and vainly attempting to articulate something — anything.

"This ain't Sonoma Valley," he declared finally. "This is fairyland, and you're a fairy. Mebbe I'm asleep and dreaming! I don't know. You and me don't know how to talk together, because, you see, you're a fairy and don't know nothing but good things — and I'm a man from the bad, wicked world."

Having achieved this much, he was left gasping for ideas like a stranded fish.

"And you're going to tell me about the bad, wicked world," she cried, clapping her hands. "I'm just dying to know."

He looked at her, startled, remembering the wreckage of womanhood he had encountered on the sunken ways of life. She was no fairy. She was flesh and blood, and the possibilities of wreckage were in her as they had been in him, even when he lay at his mother's breast. And there was in her eagerness to know.

"Nope," he said lightly; "this man from the bad, wicked world ain't going to tell you nothing of the kind. He's going to tell you of the good things in that world. He's going to tell you you how he loved hosses when he was a shaver, and about the first hoss he straddled, and the first hoss he owned. Hosses ain't like men. They're better. They're clean — clean all the way through and back again. And, little fairy, I want to tell you one thing — there sure ain't nothing in the world like when you're settin' a tired hoss at the end of a long day, and when you just speak, and that tired animal lifts under you willing and hustles along. Hosses! They're my long suit. I sure dote on hosses. Yep, I used to be a cowboy once."

She clapped her hands in the way that tore so delightfully to his heart and her eyes were dancing, as she exclaimed:

"A Texas cowboy! I always wanted to see one. I heard papa say once that cowboys are bowlegged. Are you?"

"I sure was a Texas cowboy," he answered, "but it was a long time ago. And I'm sure bowlegged. You see, you can't ride much when you're young and soft without getting the legs bent some. Why, I was only a three-year-old when I begun. He was a three-year-old, too, fresh-broken. I led him up alongside the fence, clumb to the top rail, and dropped on. He was a pinto, and a real devil at bucking, but I could do anything with him. I reckon he knowed I was only a little shaver. Some hosses knows lots more'n you think."

For half an hour Ross Shanklin rambled on with his horse reminiscences. Then came a woman's voice.

"Joan! Joan–" it called. "Where are you, dear?"

The little girl answered; and Ross Shanklin saw a woman,

clad in a soft, clinging gown, come through the gate from the bungalow.

"What have you been doing all the afternoon?" the woman asked, as she came up.

"Talking, mamma," the little girl replied. "I've had a very interesting time."

Ross Shanklin scrambled to his feet and stood watchfully and awkwardly. The little girl took the mother's hand; and she, in turn, looked at him frankly and pleasantly, with a recognition of his humanness that was a new thing to him. In his mind ran the thought: "The woman who ain't afraid!" Not a hint was there of the timidity he was accustomed too see in women's eyes; and he was quite aware of his bleary-eyed forbidding appearance.

"How do you do?" She greeted him sweetly and naturally.

"How do you do, ma'am?" he responded, unpleasantly conscious of the huskiness and rawness of his voice.

"And did you have an interesting time, too?" she smiled.

"Yes, ma'am. I sure did. I was just telling your little girl about hosses."

"He was a cowboy once, mamma!" she cried.

The mother smiled her acknowledgment to him, and looked fondly down at the little girl.

"You'll have to come along, dear," the mother said. "It's growing late." She looked at Ross Shanklin hesitantly. "Would you care to have something to eat?"

"No ma'am thanking you kindly just the same. I — I ain't hungry."

"Then say good-bye, Joan" she said.

"Goodbye!" The little girl held out her hand, and her eyes lighted roguishly. "Goodbye, Mr. Man from the bad, wicked world."

To him, the touch of her hand as he pressed it in his was the capstone of the whole adventure.

"Goodbye, little fairy!" he mumbled. "I reckon I got to be pullin' along."

But he did not pull along. He stood staring after his vision until it vanished through the gate. The day seemed suddenly empty. He looked about him irresolutely, then climbed the fence, crossed the bridge, and slouched along the road.

A mile farther on he aroused at the crossroads. Before him stood the saloon. He came to a stop and stared at it, licking his lips. He sank his hand into his pant's pocket, and pulled out a solitary dime. "God!" he muttered. "God!" Then, with dragging, reluctant feet, went on along the road.

He came to a big farm. He knew it must be big because of the bigness of the house, and the size and number of the barns and outbuildings. On the porch, in shirtsleeves, smoking a cigar, keen-eyed and middle-aged, was the farmer.

"What's the chance for a job?" Ross Shanklin asked.

The keen eyes scarcely glanced at him.

"A dollar a day and grub," was the answer.

Ross Shanklin swallowed and braced himself.

"I'll pick grapes all right, or anything. But what's the chance for a steady job? You've got a big ranch here. I know hosses. I was born on one. I can drive team, ride, plow, break, do anything that anybody ever done with hosses."

"You don't look it," was the judgment.

"I know I don't. Give me a chance — that's all. I'll prove it."

The farmer considered, casting an anxious glance at the cloudbank into which the sun had sunk.

"I'm short of a teamster, and I'll give you the chance to make good. Go and get supper with the hands."

Ross Shanklin's voice was very husky and he spoke with an effort.

"All right. I'll make good. Where can I get a drink of water and wash up?"

"The Princess"

Little information is available about the composition and publication of this story. Charmian London does mention, however, that London was in a highly-charged mood as he wrote it. She states that the "denouement is founded upon on after-dinner story once told at our table by a Bohemian clubman, an inimitable raconteur. Jack seemed to enjoy making this tale, and could hardly wait each day to catch me with his 'Come on and see how it goes'" (The Book of Jack London, II, p. 365).

A fire burned cheerfully in the jungle-camp, and beside the fire lolled a cheerful-seeming though horrible-appearing man. This was a hobo jungle, pitched in a thin strip of woods that lay between a railroad embankment and the bank of a river. But no hobo was the man. So deep-sunk was he in the social abyss that a proper hobo would not sit by the same fire with him. A gay-cat, who is an ignorant newcomer on the "road," might sit with such as he, but only long enough to learn better.

He was truly horrible-appearing. He might have been sixty years of age; he might have been ninety. His garments might have been discarded by a ragpicker. Beside him, an unrolled bundle showed itself as consisting of a ragged overcoat and containing an empty and smoke-blackened tomato-can, an empty and battered condensed-milk can, some dog-meat partly wrapped in brown paper and evidently begged from some butcher shop, a carrot that had been run over in the street by a wagon-wheel, three greenish-cankered and decayed potatoes, and a sugar bun with a mouthful bitten from it and rescued from the gutter.

Source: *Cosmopolitan,* LXV (June 1918), 20-27, 145-149.

A prodigious growth of whiskers, grayish dirty and untrimmed for years, sprouted from his face. This hirsute growth should have been white, but the season was summer and it had not been exposed to a rain-shower for some time. What was visible of the face looked as if, at some period, it had stopped a hand-grenade. The nose was so variously malformed in its healed brokenness that there was no bridge, while one nostril, the size of a pea, opened downward, and the other, the size of a robin's egg, tilted upward to the sky. One eye, of normal size, dim brown and misty, bulged to the verge of popping out, and, as if from senility, wept copiously and continuously. The other eye, scarcely larger than a squirrel's and as uncannily bright, twisted up obliquely into the hairy scar of a bone-crushed eyebrow. And he had but one arm.

Yet was he cheerful. On his face, in mild degree, was depicted sensuous pleasure as he lethargically scratched his ribs with his one hand. He pawed over his food-scraps, debated, then drew a twelve-ounce druggist's bottle from his inside coat pocket. The bottle was full of a colorless liquid, the contemplation of which made his little eye burn brighter and quickened his movements. Picking up the tomato-can, he rose, went down the short path to the river, and returned with the can filled with not-nice river water. In the condensed-milk can he mixed one part of water with two parts of fluid from the bottle. This colorless fluid was druggist's alcohol, and as such is known in tramp-land as "alki."

Slow footsteps, coming down the side of the railroad embankment, alarmed him ere he could drink. Placing the can carefully upon the ground between his legs, he covered it with his hat and waited anxiously whatever impended.

Out of the darkness emerged a man as filthy-ragged as he. The newcomer, who might have been fifty or might have been sixty, was grotesquely fat. He bulged everywhere. He was composed of bulges. His bulbous nose was the size and shape of a turnip. His eyelids bulged, and his blue eyes bulged in competition with them. In many places, the seams of his garments had parted across the bulges of his body. His calves grew into his feet, for the broken elastic sides of his congress gaiters were swelled full with the fat of him. One arm only he sported, from the shoulder of which was suspended a small and tattered bundle with the mud caked dry on the outer covering from the last place he had pitched his doss. He advanced with tentative caution, made sure of the harmlessness of the man beside the fire, and joined him.

"Hello, grandpa!" the newcomer greeted, then paused to stare at the other's flaring, sky-open nostril. "Say, Whiskers, how 'd ye keep the night dew out of that nose o' yourn?"

Whiskers growled an incoherence deep in his throat, and spat into the fire in token that he was not pleased with the question.

"For the love o' Mike!" the fat man chuckled, "If you got caught out in a rain-storm without an umbrella, you'd sure drown, wouldn't you?"

"Can it, Fatty; can it," Whiskers muttered wearily. "They ain't nothin' new in that line of chatter. Even the bulls hand it out to me."

"But you can still drink, I hope," Fatty at the same time mollified and invited, with his one hand deftly pulling the slip-knots that fastened his bundle.

From within the bundle he brought to light a twelve-ounce bottle of alki. Footsteps coming down the embankment alarmed him, and he hid the bottle under his hat on the ground between his legs.

But the next comer proved to be not merely one of their own ilk but likewise to have only one arm. So forbidding of aspect was he that greetings consisted of no more than grunts. Huge-boned, tall, gaunt to cadaverousness, his face a dirty death's-head, he was as repellent a nightmare of old age as ever Doré imagined. His toothless, thin-lipped mouth was a cruel and bitter slash under a great curved nose that almost met the chin and that was like a buzzard's beak. His one hand, lean and crooked, was a talon. The beady gray eyes, unblinking and unwavering, were bitter as death, as bleak as absolute zero, and as merciless. His presence was a chill, and Whiskers and Fatty instinctively drew together for protection against the unguessed threat of him. Watching his chance privily, Whiskers snuggled a chunk of rock several pounds in weight close to his hand, if need for action should arise. Fatty duplicated the performance.

Then both sat licking their lips, guiltily embarrassed, while the unblinking eyes of the terrible one bored now into one, now into another, and then down at the rock chunks of their pre-paredness.

"Huh!" sneered the terrible one, with such dreadfulness of menace as to cause Whiskers and Fatty involuntarily to close their hands down on their caveman's weapons. "Huh!" he repeated. reaching his one talon into his side coat pocket with swift definite-ness. "A big chance you two cheap bums'd have with me."

The talon emerged, clutching ready for action a six-pound iron quoit.

"We ain't lookin' for trouble, Slim," Fatty quavered.

"Who are you to call me 'Slim?' " came the snarling answer.

"Me? I'm just Fatty, an' seein' 's I never seen you before —"

"An' I suppose that 's Whiskers, there, with the gay an' festive lamp tangoing into his eyebrow an' the God-forgive-us nose joy-riding all over his mug?"

"It 'll do; it 'll do," Whiskers muttered uncomfortably. "One monniker's as good as another, I find, at my time of life. And everybody hands it out to me, anyway. And I need an umbrella when it rains to keep from gettin' drowned, an' all the rest of it."

"I ain't used to company — don't like it," Slim growled. "So, if you guys want to stick around, mind your step — that's all — mind your step."

He fished from his pocket a cigar stump, and prepared to put it in his mouth to chew. Then he changed his mind, glared at his companions savagely, and unrolled his bundle. Appeared in his hand a druggist's bottle of alki.

"Well," he snarled, "I suppose I gotta give you cheap skates a drink when I ain't got more 'n enough for a good petrification for myself."

Almost a softening flicker of light was imminent in his withered face as he beheld the others proudly lift their hats and exhibit their own supplies.

"Here's some water for the mixin's," Whiskers said, proffering his tomato-can.

Yet, when all was ready, cans of alki in their solitary hands, the three things that had once been men hesitated, as if of old habit, and next betrayed shame, as if at self-exposure.

Whiskers was the first to brazen it.

"I've sat in at many a finer drinking," he bragged.

"With the pewter?" Slim sneered.

"With the silver," Whiskers corrected.

Slim turned a scorching eye-interrogation on Fatty.

Fatty nodded.

"Beneath the salt," said Slim.

"Above it," came Fatty's correction. "I was born above it, and I've never traveled second class. First or steerage, but no intermediate in mine."

"Yourself?" Whiskers queried of Slim.

"I've broken glass to the queen, God bless her!" Slim answered solemnly, without snarl or sneer.

"In the pantry?" Fatty insinuated.

Simultaneously, Slim reached for his quoit and Whiskers and Fatty for their rocks.

"Now, don't let's get feverish," Fatty said, dropping his own weapon. "We aren't scum. We're gentlemen. Let's drink like gentlemen."

"Let it be a real drinking," Whiskers approved.

"Let's get petrified," Slim agreed. "Many a distillery has flowed under the bridge since we were gentlemen; but let's forget the long road we've traveled since, and hit our doss in the good old fashion in which every gentleman went to bed when we were young."

"My father done it — did it," Fatty concurred and corrected, as old recollections exploded long-sealed brain-cells of connotation and correct usage.

The other two nodded a descent from similar fathers and elevated their tin cans of alcohol.

By the time each had finished his own bottle and from his rags fished forth a second one, their brains were well mellowed and aglow, although they had not got round to telling their real names. But their English had improved. They spoke it correctly, while the *argot* of tramp-land ceased from their lips.

"It's my constitution," Whiskers was explaining, "Very few men could go through what I have and live to tell the tale. And I never took any care of myself. If what the moralists and the physiologists say is true I'd have been dead long ago. And it's the same with you two. Look at us, at our advanced years, carousing as the young ones don't dare, sleeping out in the open on the ground, never sheltered from frost or rain or storm, never afraid of pneumonia or rheumatism that would put half the young ones on their backs in hospital."

He broke off to mix another drink, and Fatty took up the tale.

"And we've had our fun," he boasted. "And speaking of sweethearts and all," he cribbed from Kipling, "we've rogued and we've ranged —' "

" 'In our time.' " Slim completed the crib for him.

"I should say so; I should say so," Fatty confirmed. "And been loved by princesses — at least, I have."

"Go on and tell us about it," Whiskers urged. "The night's young, and why shouldn't we remember back to the roofs of kings?"

Nothing loath, Fatty cleared his throat for the recital, and cast about in his mind for the best way to begin.

"It must be known that I came of good family. Percival Delany, let us say— yes: let us say Percival Delaney — was not unknown at Oxford once upon a time — not for scholarship, I am frank to admit; but the gay young dogs of that day, if any be yet alive, would remember him —"

"My people came over with the Conqueror." Whiskers interrupted, extending his hand to Fatty's in acknowledgment of the introduction.

"What name?" Fatty queried. "I did not seem quite to catch it."

"Delarouse — Chauncey Delarouse. The name will serve as well as any."

Both completed the hand-shake and glanced to Slim.

"Oh, well, while we're about it — " Fatty urged.

"Bruce Cadogan Cavendish," Slim growled morosely. "Go on, Percival, with your princesses and the roofs of kings."

"Oh, I was a rare young devil," Percival obliged, "after I played ducks and drakes at home and sported out over the world. And I was some figure of a man before I lost my shape — polo, steeplechasing, boxing, wrestling, swimming. I won medals at buck-jumping in Australia, and I held more than several swimming records from the quarter of a mile up. Women turned their heads to look when I went by. The women! God bless them!"

And Fatty, alias Percival Delaney, a grotesque of manhood, put his bulgy hand to his puffed lips and kissed audibly into the starry vault of the sky.

"And the princess," he resumed, with another kiss to the stars. "She was as fine a figure of a woman as I was a man, as high-spirited and courageous, as reckless and daredevilish. Lord, Lord, in the water she was a mermaid, A sea-goddess! And when it came to blood, beside her I was *parvenu*. Her royal line traced back into the mists of antiquity.

"She was not a daughter of fair-skinned folk. Tawny golden was she, with golden-brown eyes, and her hair that fell to her knees was blue-black and straight, with just the curly, tendrilly tendency that gives to woman's hair its charm. Oh, there were no kinks in it, any more than were their kinks in the hair of her entire genealogy. For she was Polynesian, glowing, golden, lovely, and lovable — royal Polynesian."

Again he paused to kiss his hand to the memory of her, and Slim, alias Bruce Cadogan Cavendish, took advantage to interject:

"Huh! Maybe you didn't shine in scholarship, but at least you gleaned a vocabulary out of Oxford."

"And in the South Seas garnered a better vocabulary from the lexicon of Love," Percival was quick on the uptake.

"It was the island of Talofa," he went on, "meaning 'love,' the Isle of Love, and it was her island. Her father, the king, an old man, sat on his mats with paralyzed knees and drank squareface-gin all day and most of the night, out of grief, sheer grief. She, my princess, was the only issue, her brothers having been lost in their double canoe in a hurricane while coming up from a voyage to Samoa. And among the Polynesians the royal women have equal right with the men to rule. In fact, they trace their geneal-ogies always by the female line."

To this, both Chauncey Delarouse and Bruce Cadogan Cav-endish nodded prompt affirmation.

"Ah," said Percival, "I perceive you both know the South Seas, wherefore, without undue expenditure of verbiage on my part, I am assured that you will appreciate the charm of my princess, the Princess Tui-nui, of Talofa, the princess of the Isle of Love."

He kissed his hand to her, sipped from his condensed-milk can a man-size drink of druggist's alcohol, and to her again kissed his hand.

"But she was coy, and ever she fluttered near to me but never near enough. When my arm went out to her to girdle her, presto! she was not there. I knew, as never before or since, the thousand dear and delightful anguishes of love frustrate but ever resilient and beckoned on by the very goddess of love."

"Some vocabulary," Bruce Cadogan Cavendish muttered in aside to Chauncey Delarouse. But Percival Delaney was not to be deterred. He kissed his pudgy hand aloft into the night and held warmly on.

"No fond agonies of rapture deferred that were not lavished upon me by my dear princess, herself ever a luring delight of promise flitting just beyond my reach. Every sweet lover's inferno unguessed of by Dante she led me through. Ah, those tropic nights! Those swooning tropic nights, under our palm trees, the distant surf a languorous murmur as from some vast sea-shell of mystery, when she, my princess, all but melted to my yearning, and with her laughter, that was as silver strings by buds and blossoms smitten, all but made lunacy of my lover's ardency.

"It was by my wrestling with the champions of Talofa that I first interested her. It was by my prowess at swimming that I awoke her. And it was by a certain swimming deed that I won from her more than coquettish smiles and shy timidities of feigned retreat.

"We were squidding that day, out on the reef — you know how, undoubtedly — diving down the face of the wall of the reef, five fathoms, ten fathoms, any depth within reason, and shoving our squid-sticks into the likely holes and crannies of the coral where squid might be lairing. With the squid-stick, bluntly sharp at both ends, perhaps a foot long and held crosswise in the hand, the trick was to gouge any lazying squid until he closed his tentacles around fist, stick, and arm. Then you had him, and came to the surface with him, and peeled him off into the waiting canoe — and to think I used to do that!"

Percival Delaney paused a moment, a glimmer of awe on his rotund face as he contemplated the mighty picture of his youth.

"Why, I've pulled out a squid with tentacles eight feet long, and done it under fifty feet of water. I could stay down four minutes. I've gone down, with a coral rock to sink me, in a hundred and ten feet to clear a fouled anchor. And I could back-dive with a once-over and go in feet first from eighty feet above the surface — "

"Quit it; delete it; cease it!" Chauncey Delarouse admonished testily. "Tell of the princess. That's what makes old blood leap again. Almost can I see her. Was she very wonderful?"

Percival Delaney kissed unutterable affirmation.

"I have said she was a mermaid. She was. I know she swam thirty-six hours before being rescued, after her schooner was capsized in a double squall. I have seen her do ninety feet and bring up pearl-shells in each hand. She *was* wonderful. As a woman, she was ravishing, sublime. I have said she was a sea-goddess. She was. Oh, for a Phidias or a Praxiteles to have made the wonder of her body immortal!

"And that day, out for squid on the reef, I was almost sick for her. Mad — I know I was mad for her. We would step over the side from the big canoe, and swim down, side by side, into the delicious depths of cool and color, and she would look at me as we swam, and with her eyes tantalize me to further madness. And at last, down, far down, I lost myself and reached for her. She eluded me like the mermaid she was, and I saw the laughter on her face as she fled. She fled deeper, and I knew I had her, for I was between her and the surface; but, in the muck coral sand of the bottom, she made a churning with her squid-stick. It was the old trick to escape a shark. And she worked it on me, roiling the water so that I could not see her. And when I came up, she was there ahead of me, clinging to the side of the canoe and laughing.

"Almost I would not be denied. But not for nothing was she a princess. She rested her hand on my arm and compelled me to listen. We should play a game, she said, enter into a competition for which should get the more squid, the biggest squid, and the smallest squid. Since the wagers were kisses, you can well imagine I went down on the first next dive with soul aflame.

"I got no squid. Never again in my life have I dived for squid. Perhaps we were five fathoms down and exploring the face of the reef wall for lurking-places of our prey when it happened. I had found a likely lair and just proved it empty, when I felt, or sensed, the nearness of something inimical. I turned. There it was, alongside of me, and no mere fish-shark. Fully a dozen feet in length, with the unmistakable phosphorescent cat's eye gleaming like a drowning star, I knew it for what it was, a tigershark.

"Not ten feet away, probing a coral fissure with her squid-stick, was the princess, and the tigershark was heading directly for her. My totality of thought was precipitated to consciousness in a single, all-embracing flash. The man-eater must be deflected from her, and what was I, except a mad lover who would gladly fight and die, or more gladly fight and live, for his beloved?

"Knowing fully the peril of my act, I thrust the blunt-sharp end of my squid-stick into the side of the shark, much as one would attract a passing acquaintance with a thumb-nudge in the ribs. And the man-eater turned on me. You know the South Seas, and you know that the tigershark, like the bald-face grizzly of Alaska, never gives trail. The combat, fathoms deep under the sea, was on — if by combat may be named such a one-sided struggle.

"The princess, unaware, caught her squid and rose to the surface. The man-eater rushed me. I fended him off with both hands on his nose above his thousand-toothed open mouth, so that he backed me against the sharp coral. The scars are there to this day. Whenever I tried to rise, he rushed me, and I could not remain there down indefinitely without air. Whenever he rushed me, I fended off with my hands on his nose. And I would have escaped unharmed except for the slip of my right hand. Into his mouth it went to the elbow. His jaws closed, just below the elbow. You know how a shark's teeth are. Once in, they cannot be released. They must go through to complete the bite, but they cannot go through heavy bone. So, from just below the elbow, he stripped the bone clean to the articulation of the wrist-joint, where his teeth met and my good right hand became his for an appetizer.

"But while he was doing this, I drove the thumb of my left hand, to the hilt, into his eye-orifices and popped out his eye. This did not stop him. The meat had maddened him. He pursued the gushing stump of my wrist. Half a dozen times I fended with my intact arm. Then he got the poor mangled arm again, closed down, and stripped the meat off the bone from the shoulder down to the elbow-joint, where his teeth met and he was free of his second mouthful of me. But, at the same time, with my good arm, I thumbed out his remaining eye."

Percival Delaney shrugged his shoulders, ere he resumed.

"From above, those in the canoe had beheld the entire happening and were loud in praise of my deed. To this day, they still sing the song of me, and tell the tale of me. And the princess" — his pause was brief but significant — "the princess married me. Oh, welladay and lackaday, the whirligig of time and fortune, the topsyturviness of luck, the wooden shoe going up and the polished heel descending, a French gunboat, a conquered island-kingdom of Oceania, to-day ruled over by a peasant-born, unlettered, colonial gendarme, and— "

He completed the sentence and the tale by burying his face in the down-tilted mouth of the condensed-milk can and by gurgling the corrosive drink down his throat in thirsty gulps.

After an appropriate pause, Chauncey Delarouse, otherwise Whiskers, took up the tale.

"Far be it from me to boast of no matter what place of birth I have descended from to sit here by this fire with such as — as chance along. I may say, however, that I, too, was once a considerable figure of a man. I may add that it was horses, plus parents too indulgent, that exiled me out over the world. I may still wonder to query, 'Are Dover's cliffs still white?' "

"Huh!" Bruce Cadogan Cavendish sneered. "Next you'll be asking, 'How fares the old Lord Warden?' "

"And I took every liberty, and vainly, with a constitution that was iron," Whiskers hurried on. "Here I am, with my three-score and ten behind me, and back on that long road have I buried many a youngster that was as rare and devilish as I but who could not stand the pace. I knew the worst too young. And now I know the worst too old. But there was a time —alas, all too short! — when I knew the best.

"I, too, kiss my hand to the princess of my heart. She was truly a princess, Polynesian, a thousand miles and more away to the eastward and the south from Delaney's Isle of Love. The natives of all round that part of the South Seas called it the 'Jolly Island.' Their own name, the name of the people who dwelt thereon, translates delicately and justly into the 'Island of Tranquil Laughter.' On the chart you will find the erroneous name given to it by the old navigators to be Manatomana. The seafaring gentry the round ocean round called it the 'Adamless Eden.' And the missionaries for a time called it 'God's Witness' — so great had been their success at converting the inhabitants. As for me, it was, and ever shall be, paradise.

"It was *my* paradise, for it was there my princess lived. John Asibeli Tungi was king. He was a full-blooded native, descended out of the oldest and highest chief-stock that traced back to Manua, which was the primeval sea-home of the race. Also, was he known as 'John the Apostate.' He lived a long life and apostasized frequently. First converted by the Catholics, he threw down the idols, broke the tabus, cleaned out the native priests, executed a few of the recalcitrant ones, and sent all his subjects to church.

"Next he fell for the traders, who developed in him a champagne thirst, and he shipped off the Catholic priests to New Zealand. The great majority of his subjects always followed his lead, and, having no religion at all, ensued the time of the Great Licentiousness, when, by all South Seas missionaries, his island, in sermons, was spoken of as 'Babylon.'

"But the traders ruined his digestion with too much champagne, and after several years he fell for the Gospel according to the Methodists, sent his people to church, and cleaned up the beach and the trading crowd so spick and span that he would not permit them to smoke a. pipe out of doors on Sunday, and fined one of the chief traders a hundred gold sovereigns for washing his schooner's decks on the Sabbath morn.

"That was the time of the blue laws, but perhaps it was too rigorous for King John. Off he packed the Methodists, one fine day, exiled several hundred of his people to Samoa for sticking to Methodism, and, of all things, invented a religion of his own, with himself the figurehead of worship. In this, he was aided, and abetted by a renegade Fijian. This lasted five years. Maybe he grew tired of being God, or maybe it was because the Fijian decamped with the six thousand pounds in the royal treasury, but, at any rate, the Second Reformed Wesleyans got him and his entire kingdom went Wesleyan. The pioneer Wesleyan missionary he actually made prime minister, and what he did to the trading crowd was a caution. Why, in the end, King John's kingdom was blacklisted and boycotted by the traders till the revenues diminished to zero, the people went bankrupt, and King John couldn't borrow a shilling from his most powerful chief.

"By this time he was getting old and philosophic and tolerant and spiritually atavistic. He fired out the Second Reformed Wesleyans, called back the exiles from Samoa, invited in the traders, held a general love-feast, took the lid off, proclaimed religious liberty and high tariff, and, as for himself, went back to the worship of his ancestors, dug up the idols, reinstated a few octogenarian priests, and observed the tabus. All of which was lovely for the traders, and prosperity reigned. Of course, most of his subjects followed him back into the heathen worship. Yet quite a sprinkling of Catholics, Methodists, and Wesleyans remained true to their beliefs and managed to maintain a few squalid, one-horse churches. But King John didn't mind, any more than he did the high times of the traders along the beach. Everything went, so long as the taxes were paid. Even when his wife, Queen Mamare, elected to become a Baptist, and invited in a little wizened, sweet-spirited, club-footed Baptist missionary, King John did not object. All he insisted on was that these wandering religions should be self-supporting and not feed a pennyworth out of the royal coffers.

"And now the threads of my recital draw together in the paragon of female exquisiteness — my princess."

Whiskers paused, placed carefully on the ground his half-full condensed-milk can, with which he had been absently toying, and kissed the fingers of his one hand audibly aloft.

"She was the daughter of Queen Mamare. She was the woman wonderful. Unlike the Diana type of Polynesian, she was almost ethereal. She *was* ethereal, subliminated by purity, as shy and modest as a violet, as fragile-slender as a lily, and her eyes, luminous and shrinking-tender, were as asphodels on the sward of heaven. She was all flower and fire and dew. Hers was the sweetness of the mountain-rose, the gentleness of the dove.

And she was all of good as well as all of beauty, devout in her belief in her mother's worship, which was the worship introduced by Ebenezer Naismith, the Baptist missionary. But make no mistake—she was no mere sweet spirit ripe for the bosom of Abraham. All of exquisite deliciousness of woman was she. She was woman, all woman, to the last sensitive quivering atom of her.

"And I — I was a wastrel of the beach. The wildest was not so wild as I, the keenest not so keen, of all that wild, keen, trading crowd. It was esteemed I played the stiffest hand of poker. I was the only living man, white, brown, or black, who dared run the Kuni-kuni Passage in the dark. And on a black night I have done it under reefs in a gale of wind. Well, anyway, I had a bad reputation on a beach where there were no good reputations. I was reckless, dangerous, stopped at nothing in fight or frolic; and the trading captains used to bring boiler-sheeted prodigies from the vilest holes of the South Pacific to try and drink me under the table. I remember one, a calcined Scotchman from the New Hebrides. It was a great drinking. He died of it, and we laded him aboard ship, pickled in a cask of trade-rum, and sent him back to his own place. A sample, a fair sample, of the antic tricks we cut up on the beach of Manatomana.

"And of all unthinkable things, what did I up and do, one day, but look upon the princess to find her good and to fall in love with her. It was the real thing. I was as mad as a March hare, and, after that, I got only madder. I reformed. Think of that! Think of what a slip of a woman can do to a lusty, roving man! By the Lord Harry, it's true! I reformed. I went to church. Hear me! I became converted. I cleared my soul before God and kept my hands — I had two of then — off the ribald crew of the beach when it laughed at this, my latest antic, and wanted to know what was my game.

"I tell you I reformed, and gave myself in passion and sincerity to a religious experience that has made me tolerant of all religion ever since. I discharged my best captain for immorality. So did I my cook, and a better never boiled water in Manatomana. For the same reason, I discharged my chief clerk. And, for the first time in the history of trading, my schooners to the westward carried Bibles in their stock. I built a little anchorite bungalow up-town on a mango-lined street, squarely alongside the little house occupied by Ebenezer Naismith. And I made him my pal and comrade, and found him a veritable honey-pot of sweetnesses and goodnesses. And he was a man — through and through a man. And he died long after like a man, which I would like to tell you about, were the tale of it not so deservedly long.

"It was the princess, more than the missionary, who was responsible for my expressing my faith in works, and especially in that crowning work, the new church, our church, the queen-mother's church.

" 'Our poor church,' the princess said to me, one night after prayer-meeting. I had been converted only a fortnight. 'It is so small its congregation can never grow. And the roof leaks. And King John, my hard-hearted father, will not contribute a penny. Yet he has a big balance in the treasury. And Manatomana is not poor. Much money is made and squandered. I know. I hear the gossip of the wild ways of the beach. Less than a month ago you lost more in one night, gambling at cards, than the cost of the up-keep of our poor church for a year.'

"And I told her it was true, but that it was before I had seen the light. (I'd had an infernal run of bad luck.) I told her that I had not tasted liquor since, or turned a card. I told her that the roof would be repaired at once by Christian carpenters selected by her from the congregation. But she was filled with the thought of a great revival that Ebenezer Naismith could preach — she was a dear saint — and she spoke of a great church, saying:

" 'You are rich. You have many schooners and traders in far islands, and I have heard of a great contract you have signed to recruit labor for the German plantations of Upolu. They say, next to Sweitzer, you are the richest trader here. I should love to see some use of all this money placed to the glory of God. It would be a noble thing to do, and I should be proud to know the man who would do it.'

"I told her that Ebenezer Naismith would preach the revival, and that I would build a church great enough in which to house it.

" 'As big as the Catholic Church?' she asked.

"I was afire with love, and I told her that the church I would build would be even bigger. 'But it will take money,' I explained. 'And it takes time to make money.'

" 'You have much,' she said. 'Some say you have more money than my father, the king.'

" 'I have more credit,' I explained. 'But you do not understand money. It takes money to have credit. So, with the money I have and the credit I have, I will work to make more money and credit, and the church shall be built.'

"Work! I was a surprise to myself. It is an amazement, the amount of time a man finds on his hands after he's given up carousing and gambling and all the time-eating diversions of the beach. And I didn't waste a second of all my new-found time. Instead, I worked it overtime; I did the work of half a dozen men. I became a driver. My captains made faster runs than ever and earned bigger bonuses, as did my supercargoes, who saw to it that my schooners did not loaf and dawdle along the way. And I saw to it that my supercargoes did see to it.

"And good! By the Lord Harry, I was so good it hurt! My conscience got so expansive and fine-strung it lamed me across the shoulders to carry it around with me. Why, I even went back over my accounts and paid Sweitzer fifty quid I'd jiggered him out of in a deal in Fiji three years before. And I compounded the interest as well.

"Work! I planted sugar-cane — the first commercial planting on Manatomana. I ran in cargoes of kinky-heads from Malaita, in the Solomons until I had twelve hundred of the blackbirds putting in cane. And I sent a schooner clear to Hawaii to bring back a dismantled sugar-mill and a German who said he knew the field-end of cane. And he did, and he charged me three hundred dollars screw a month, and I took hold of the mill-end. I installed the mill myself, with the help of several mechanics I brought up from Queensland.

"Of course there was a rival. His name was Motomoe. His was the very highest chief-blood next to King John's. He was full native, a strapping, handsome man with a glowering way of showing his dislikes. He certainly glowered at me when I began hanging round the palace. He went back in my history and circulated the blackest tales about me. The worst of it was that most of them were true. He even made a voyage to Apia to find things out, as if he couldn't find a plenty right there on the beach of Manatomana! And he sneered at my falling for religion, and at my going to prayer-meeting, and, most of all, at my sugar-planting. He challenged me to fight, and I kept off of him. He threatened me, and I learned in the nick of time of his plan to have me knocked on the head. You see, he wanted the princess just as much as I did, and I wanted her more.

"She used to play the piano. So did I — once. But I never let her know after I'd heard her play the first time. And she thought her playing was wonderful, the dear, fond girl! You know the sort, the mechanical one-two-three, tum-tum-tum schoolgirl stuff. And now I'll tell you something funnier. Her playing was wonderful to me. The gates of heaven opened to me when she played. I can see myself now worn out and dog-tired after the long day, lying on the mats of the palace veranda and gazing upon her at the piano, myself in a perfect idiocy of bliss. Why, this idea she had of her fine playing was the one flaw in her deliciousness of perfection, and I loved her for it. It kind of brought her within my human reach. Why, when she played her one-two-three, tum-tum-tum, I was in the seventh heaven of bliss. My weariness fell from me. I loved her, and my love for her was clean as flame, clean as my love for God. And do you know, into my fond lover's fancy continually intruded the thought that God in most ways must look like her —

"That's right, Bruce Cadogan Cavendish, sneer as you like. But I tell you that's love that I've been describing. That's all. It's love. It's the realest, purest, finest thing that can happen to a man. And I know what I'm talking about. It happened to me."

Whiskers, his beady squirrel's eye glittering from out his ruined eyebrow like a live coal in a jungle ambush, broke off long enough to down a sedative draft from his condensed-milk can and to mix another.

"The cane," he resumed, wiping his prodigious mat of face hair with the back of his hand, "it matured in sixteen months in that climate, and I was ready, just ready and no more, with the mill for the grinding. Naturally, it did not all mature at once, but I had planted in such succession that I could grind for nine months steadily, while more was being planted and the ratoons were springing up.

"I had my troubles the first several days. If it wasn't one thing the matter with the mill, it was another. On the fourth day, Ferguson, my engineer, had to shut down several hours in order to remedy his own troubles. I was bothered by the feeder. After having the niggers (who had been feeding the cane) pour cream of lime on the rollers to keep everything sweet, I sent them out to join the cane-cutting squads.

"So I was all alone at that end, just as Ferguson started up the mill, just as I discovered what was the matter with the feed-rollers, and just as Motomoe strolled up.

"He stood there, in Norfolk jacket, pigskin puttees, and all the rest of the fashionable get-up out of a bandbox, sneering at me covered with filth and grease to the eyebrows and looking like a navvy. And, the rollers now white from the lime. I'd just seen what was wrong. They were not in plumb. One side crushed the cane well, but the other side was too open. I shoved my fingers in on that side. The big, toothed cogs on the rollers did not touch my fingers. And yet, suddenly, they did. With the grip of ten thousand devils, my finger-tips were caught, drawn in, and pulped to — well, just pulp. And, like a stick of cane, I had started on my way. Ten thousand horses could not have pulled me back. There was nothing to stop me. Hand, arm, shoulder, head, and chest, down to the toes of me, I was doomed to feed through.

"It did hurt. It hurt so much it did not hurt at all. Quite detached, almost may I say, I looked on my hand being ground up, knuckle by knuckle, joint by joint, the back of my hand, the wrist, the forearm, all in order slowly and inevitably feeding in.

"Motomoe sprang forward involuntarily, and the sneer was chased from his face by an expression of solicitude. Then the beauty of the situation dawned on him, and he chuckled and grinned. No; I didn't expect anything of him. What could he do, anyway? He didn't know anything about engines.

"I yelled at the top of my lungs to Ferguson to shut off the engine, but the roar of the machinery drowned my voice. And there I stood, up to the elbow and feeding right on in. Yes; it did hurt. There were some astonishing twinges when special nerves were shredded and dragged out by the roots. But I remember that I was surprised at the time that it did not hurt more.

"Motomoe made a movement that attracted my attention. At the same time, he growled out loud, as if he hated himself, 'I'm a fool.' What he had done was to pick up a cane-knife — you know the kind, as big as a machete and as heavy. And I was grateful to him in advance for putting me out of my misery. There wasn't any sense in slowly feeding in till me head was crushed, and already my arm was pulped half-way from elbow to shoulder, and the pulping was going right on. So I was grateful. I bent my head to the blow.

" 'Get your head out of the way, you idiot!' he barked at me.

"And then I understood and obeyed. I was a big man, and he took two hacks to do it; but he hacked my arm off just outside the shoulder and dragged me back and laid me down on the cane —

"Yes; the sugar paid — enormously; and I built for the princess the church of her saintly dream, and — she married me."

He partly assuaged his thirst, and uttered his final word.

"Alackaday! Shuttlecock and battledore! And this at the end of it all, lined with boiler-plate that even alcohol will not corrode and that only alcohol will tickle. Yet have I lived, and I kiss my hand to the dear dust of my princess, long asleep in the great mausoleum of King John that looks across the Vale of Manona to the alien flag that floats over the bungalow of the British government-house."

Fatty pledged him sympathetically, drank out of his own small can. Bruce Cadogan Cavendish glared into the fire with implacable bitterness. He was a man who preferred to drink by himself. Across the thin lips that composed the cruel slash of his mouth played twitches of mockery that caught Fatty's eye. And Fatty, making sure first that his rock chunk was within reach, challenged:

"Well, how about yourself, Bruce Cadogan Cavendish? It's your turn."

"I've lived a hard life," Slim grated harshly. "What do I know about love-passages?"

"No man of your build and make-up could have escaped them," Fatty wheedled.

"And what of it?" Slim snarled. "It's no reason for a gentleman to boast of amorous triumphs."

"Oh, go on; be a good fellow!" Fatty urged. "Surely you've got at least one adventure in love you aren't ashamed to tell about."

Bruce Cadogan Cavendish pulled forth his iron quoit and seemed to debate whether or not he should brain the other. He sighed and put back the quoit.

"Very well, if you will have it," he surrendered, with manifest reluctance. "Like you two, I have had a remarkable constitution. And right now, speaking of armor-plate lining, I could drink the both of you down when you were at your prime. Like you two, my beginnings were far distant and different. That I am marked with the hall-mark of gentlehood there is no discussion — unless either of you cares to discuss the matter now." His one hand slipped into his pocket and clutched the quoit. Neither of his auditors spoke nor betrayed any awareness of his menace.

"It occurred a thousand miles to the westward of Manatomana, on the island of Tagalag," he continued abruptly, with an air of saturnine disappointment in that there had been no discussion. "But first I must tell you of how I got to Tagalag. For reasons I shall not mention, by paths of descent I shall not describe, I found myself master and owner of a schooner so well known that she shall remain historically nameless. I was running blackbird labor from the West South Pacific and the Coral Sea to the plantations of Hawaii and the nitrate mines of Chile — "

"It was you who cleaned out the entire population of — " Fatty exploded.

The one hand of Bruce Cadogan Cavendish flashed pocketward and flashed back with the quoit balanced ripe for business.

"Proceed," Fatty sighed; "I — I have quite forgotten what I was going to say."

"Beastly funny country over that way," the narrator drawled, with perfect casualness. "You've read this Sea-Wolf stuff — "

"You weren't the Sea-Wolf!" Whiskers broke in, with involuntary positiveness.

"No sir," was the snarling answer; "the Sea-Wolf's dead, isn't he? And I'm still alive, aren't I?"

"Of course, of course," Whiskers conceded. "He suffocated head first in the mud off a wharf in Victoria a couple of years back."

"As I was saying — and I don't like interruptions," Bruce Cadogan Cavendish proceeded, "it's a beastly funny country over that way. I was at Taka-tiki, a low island that politically belongs to the Solomons but that geologically doesn't at all, for the Solomons are high islands. Ethnographically, it belongs to Polynesia, Melanesia, and Micronesia, because all the breeds of the South Pacific have gravitated to it by canoe-drift and intricately, degeneratively, and amazingly interbred. The scum of the scrapings of the bottom of the human pit, biologically speaking, reside in Taka-tiki.

"It was a beastly funny time of it I had, diving out shell, fishing bêche-de-mer, trading hoop-iron and hatchets for copra and ivory-nuts, rounding niggers, and all the rest of it. Why, even in Fiji, the Lotu was having a hard time of it and the chiefs still eating long-pig. To the westward it was fierce — funny little black kinky-heads, man-eaters the last Jack of them.

"They're all head-hunters. Heads are valuable, especially a white man's head. They decorate the canoe-houses and devil-devil houses with them. Each village runs a jack pot, and everybody antes. Whoever brings in a white man's head takes the pot. If there aren't openers for a long time, the pot grows to tremendous proportions. Beastly funny, isn't it?

"I know. Didn't a Holland mate die on me of black-water? And didn't I win a pot myself? It was this way: We were lying at Lango-lui at the time. I never let on, and arranged the affair with Johnny, my boat-steerer. He was a kinky-head himself from Fort Morseby. He cut the dead mate's head off and sneaked ashore in the night, while I whanged away with my rifle as if I were trying to get him. He opened the pot with the mate's head, and got it, too. Of course, next day I sent in a landing-boat, with two covering boats, and fetched him off with the loot."

"How big was the pot?" Whiskers asked.

"To commence with," Slim answered, "there were forty fat pigs, each worth a fathom of prime shell money, and shell money worth a quid a fathom. That was two hundred dollars right there. There were ninety-eight fathoms of shell money, which is pretty close to five hundred in itself. And there were twenty-two gold sovereigns. I split it four ways: one-fourth to Johnny, one-fourth to the ship, one-fourth to me as owner, and one-fourth to me as skipper. Johnny never complained. He'd never had so much wealth all at one time in his life. Besides, I gave him a couple of the mate's old shirts. And I fancy the mate's head is still there, decorating the canoe-house."

"Not exactly Christian burial of a Christian," Whiskers observed.

"But a lucrative burial," Slim retorted. "I had to feed the rest of the mate overside to the sharks for nothing. Think of feeding an eight-hundred-dollar head along with it? It would have been criminal waste and stark lunacy.

"Well, anyway it was all beastly funny, over there to the westward. And, without telling you the scrape I got into at Taka-tiki, except that I sailed away with two hundred kinky-heads for Queensland labor, and, for my manner of collecting them, had two British ships of war combing the Pacific for me, I changed my course, and ran to the westward, thinking to dispose of the lot to the plantations on Bangar.

"Typhoon season. We caught it. The Merry Mist was my schooner's name, and I had thought she was stoutly built until she hit that typhoon. I never saw such seas. They pounded that stout craft to pieces — literally so. The sticks were jerked out of her, deck-houses splintered to match-wood, rails ripped off, and, after the worst had passed, the covering-boards began to go. We just managed to repair what was left of one boat and keep the schooner afloat only till the sea went down barely enough to get away. And we outfitted that boat in a hurry. The carpenter and I were the last, and we had to jump for it as she went down. There were only four of us — "

"Lost all the niggers?" Whiskers inquired.

"Some of them swam for some time," Slim replied. "But I don't fancy they made the land. We were ten days in doing it. And we had a spanking breeze most of the way. And what do you think we had in the boat with us? Cases of square-face gin and cases of dynamite. Funny, wasn't it? Well, it got funnier later on. Oh, there was a small breaker of water, a little salt-horse, and some salt-water-soaked sea-biscuit — enough to keep us alive to Tagalag.

"Now, Tagalag is the disappointingest island I've ever beheld. It shows up out of the sea so you can make its fall twenty miles off. It is a volcano-cone thrust up out of deep sea, with a segment of the crater wall broken out. This gives sea-entrance to the crater itself, and makes a fine sheltered harbor. And that's all. Nothing lives there. The outside and the inside of the crater are too steep. At one place, inside, is a patch of about a thousand coco-palms. And that's all, as I said, saving a few insects. No four-legged thing, even a rat, inhabits the place. And it's funny, most awful funny, with all those coconuts, not even a coconut-crab. The only meat-food living was schools of mullet in the harbor — fattest, finest, biggest mullet I ever laid eyes on.

"And the four of us landed on the little beach and set up housekeeping among the coconuts with a larder full of dynamite and square-face. Why don't you laugh? It's funny, I tell you. Try it some time — Holland gin and straight coconut diet. I've never been able to look a confectioners' window in the face since.

Now, I'm not strong on religion, like Chauncey Delarouse there, but I have some primitive ideas, and my concept of hell is an illimitable coconut plantation stocked with cases of square-face and populated by shipwrecked mariners. Funny? It would make the devil scream.

"You know, straight coconut is what the agriculturists call an unbalanced ration. It certainly unbalanced our digestions. We got so that, whenever hunger took an extra bite at us, we took another drink of gin. After a couple of weeks of it, Olaf, a square-head sailor, got an idea. It came when he was full of gin, and we, being in the same fix, just watched him shove a cap and short fuse into a stick of dynamite and stroll down toward the boat.

"It dawned on me that he was going to shoot fish if there were any about; but the sun was beastly hot, and I just reclined there and hoped he'd have luck.

"About half an hour after he disappeared, we heard the explosion. But he didn't come back. We waited till the cool of the sunset, and down on the beach found what had become of him. The boat was there all right, grounded by the prevailing breeze, but there was no Olaf. He would never have to eat coconut again. We went back, shakier than ever, and cracked another square-face.

"The next day, the cook announced that he would rather take his chance with dynamite than continue trying to exist on coconut, and that, though he didn't know anything about dynamite, he knew a sight too much about coconut. So we bit the detonator down for him, shoved in a fuse, and picked him a good fire-stick, while he jolted up with a couple more stiff ones of gin.

"It was the same program as the day before. After a while, we heard the explosion, and at twilight went down to the boat, from which we scraped enough of the cook for a funeral.

"The carpenter and I stuck it out two days more; then we drew straws for it, and it was his turn. We parted with harsh words; for he wanted to take a square-face along to refresh himself by the way, while I was set against running any chance of wasting the gin. Besides, he had more than he could carry then, and he wobbled and staggered as he walked.

"Same thing — only there was a whole lot of him left for me to bury, because he's prepared only half a stick. I managed to last it out till next day, when, after duly fortifying myself, I got sufficient courage to tackle the dynamite. I used only a third of a stick — you know, short fuse, with the end split so as to hold the head of a safety-match. That's where I mended my predecessor's methods. Not using the match-head, they had too long fuses. Therefore, when they spotted a school of mullet and lighted the fuse, they had to hold the dynamite till the fuse burned short before they threw it. If they threw it too soon, it wouldn't go off the instant it hit the water, while the splash of it would frighten the mullet away.

"I picked up a school of mullet before I'd been rowing five minutes. Fine, big, fat ones they were, and I could smell them over the fire. When I stood up, fire-stick in one hand, dynamite stick in the other, my knees were knocking together. Twice I failed to touch the fire-stick to the dynamite. Then I did, and let her go.

"Now, I don't know what happened to the others, but I know what I did. I got turned about. Did you ever stem a strawberry and throw the strawberry away and pop the stem into your mouth? That's what I did. I threw the fire-stick into the water after the mullet and held onto the dynamite. And my arm went off with the stick when it went off."

Slim investigated the tomato-can for water to mix himself a drink, but found it empty. He stood up.

"Heigh-ho!" he yawned, and started down the path to the river. In several minutes he was back. He mixed the due quantity of river-water with the alcohol, took a long, solitary drink, and stared with bitter moodiness into the fire.

"Yes, but — " Fatty suggested, "what happened then?"

"Oh!" said Slim. "Then the princess married me, of course."

"But you were the only person left, and there wasn't any princess!" Whiskers cried out abruptly, and then let his voice trail away to embarrassed silence.

Slim stared unblinkingly into the fire.

Percival Delaney and Chauncey Delarouse looked at each other. Quietly, in solemn silence, each with his one arm aided the one arm of the other in rolling and tying his bundle. And in silence, bundles slung on shoulders, they went away out of the circle of firelight. Not until they reached the top of the railroad embankment did they speak.

"No gentleman would have done it," said Whiskers.

"No gentleman would have done it," Fatty agreed.

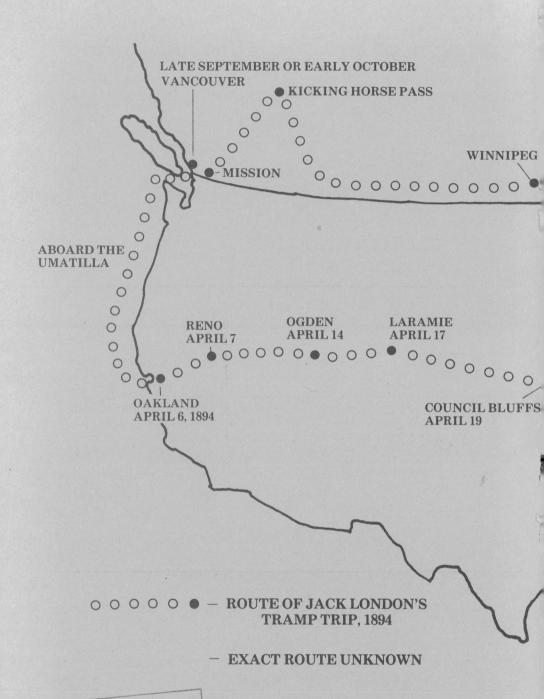

LATE SEPTEMBER OR EARLY OCTOBER
VANCOUVER
● KICKING HORSE PASS

WINNIPEG

●—MISSION

ABOARD THE
UMATILLA

RENO
APRIL 7

OGDEN
APRIL 14

LARAMIE
APRIL 17

OAKLAND
APRIL 6, 1894

COUNCIL BLUFFS
APRIL 19

○ ○ ○ ○ ○ ● — **ROUTE OF JACK LONDON'S TRAMP TRIP, 1894**

— **EXACT ROUTE UNKNOWN**